# FUN THINGS TO DO IN RETIREMENT

## IGNITE PASSION, EMBRACE FUN, AND CREATE YOUR DREAM LIFE ON A BUDGET

RHONDA GUDGER

*This book is dedicated to my family, Nancy and Heather, whose support and love know no bounds. It is also for those on the verge of starting their retirement journey, those who are already enjoying this chapter of life, and the kind-hearted individuals assisting others in preparing for this significant transition. May this book serve as a guide and inspiration for all.*

# CONTENTS

# INTRODUCTION

---

*"Retirement is a blank sheet of paper. It is a chance to redesign your life into something new and different."*

### PATRICK FOLEY

---

So, you've probably heard the old retirement dream a million times—something about sipping piña coladas on a sun-soaked beach, right? Well, hold onto your straw hats because we're about to shake up that coconut tree!

This isn't just another retirement guide; it's your ticket to an exhilarating adventure beyond the beach. You see, my husband and I are on the cusp of this incredible life chapter ourselves, with his retirement looming just five years away. And let me tell you, we haven't been sitting around waiting for the retirement fairy to sprinkle us with magical dust. We've been on a mission—researching, planning, and compiling a list of activities that promise a retirement filled with joy, purpose, and a good dose of laughter.

This book is our labor of love, born from our proactive quest to uncover the most fulfilling, vibrant, and, importantly, budget-friendly ways to spend our golden years. We're not just talking about filling time here but redefining retirement. My goal in writing this book? I hope it will ignite your passions (both new and old), embrace fun like never before, and see every day as an opportunity for exploration.

Now, this isn't your run-of-the-mill retirement manual. We're bringing humor to the table, spicing up practical advice with anecdotes, witty insights, and a healthy sprinkle of light-hearted banter. We've got you covered, from tech exploration to physical endeavors to travel hacks and everything in between. Whether you're a tech whiz or someone who thinks "Twitter" is the sound birds make in the morning, there's something in here for you.

There will be laughs along the way — but we're also serious about helping you craft an extraordinary retirement. Each chapter is packed with real-world examples, actionable steps, and tips to dive headfirst into the activities we discuss. Plus, we've organized the book into bite-sized sections, making it easy to jump around and find exactly what tickles your fancy at any given moment.

So, this book is for you whether you're counting down the days until retirement, already dancing in its glory, or helping a loved one navigate this exciting phase. We're here to show you that retirement is not just a time to relax but a time to live fully, learn eagerly, and laugh often.

And just to keep things lively, we've added some fun pics, quotes and jokes.

# CHAPTER 1

# USING DIGITAL TOOLS FOR YOUR ADVENTURES

---

*"Technology, like art, is a soaring exercise of the human imagination."*

*DANIEL BILL*

---

Some of us are tech-savvy regarding our computers, tablets, and smartphones. Others spend hours at the Apple bar or on YouTube trying to figure out the new tech. No matter our bias, there's no question that some basic use of technology, such as social media and other apps, will aid in capturing your photos, learning a new  skill, or coordinating your family's travel. This chapter covers these topics and more.

## 1.1 CAPTURING LIFE'S MOMENTS: PHOTOGRAPHY WITH YOUR SMARTPHONE

Gone are the days when capturing life's magic moments required bulky cameras and rolls of film that needed developing. Today, the power to freeze time rests snugly in our pockets or purses, thanks to smartphones. Remarkably, these devices have democratized photography, turning us all into potential shutterbugs capable of capturing, editing, and sharing moments with a device that also makes phone calls. But here's the rub: with great power comes the great responsibility of knowing how to use it.

Fear not; this isn't about turning you into the next Ansel Adams; it's about helping you wield your smartphone's camera like a pro to capture the everyday wonders, making sure those golden memories are just a swipe away.

The first step to mastering smartphone photography is getting acquainted with your device's camera. It's easy to fall into the trap of thinking more about the next photo opportunity than understanding the tool in your hands. Yet, the truth is, unlocking your smartphone camera's potential is the basics to learning how to drive: intimidating at first but liberating once you get the hang of it.

## UNDERSTANDING YOUR SMARTPHONE CAMERA

Every smartphone camera comes with a variety of settings and modes, from portrait and landscape to night and panorama. The key to using them effectively lies in understanding what each setting does. For instance, the HDR (High Dynamic Range) mode captures a series of photos at different exposures and combines them to create a single image with enhanced detail in shadows and highlights. It's perfect for scenes with a mix of bright and dark areas. Meanwhile, the rule of thirds, a principle that suggests dividing the frame into nine equal segments, can be easily applied using the grid feature on your camera, turning ordinary shots into well-composed masterpieces.

Experiment with these settings. Next time you're out for an evening walk, try the night mode to capture the subtle interplay of shadows and streetlights. You'll be surprised at how a basic understanding of your smartphone's capabilities can elevate your photos from good to breathtaking.

## CREATIVE PHOTOGRAPHY TIPS

The beauty of smartphone photography lies in its spontaneity. Yet, a sprinkle of creativity can turn spur-of-the-moment shots into lasting memories. Consider the lighting; natural light, especially during the golden hour – shortly after sunrise or before sunset – can add a magical quality to your photos. Play with angles, too; sometimes, capturing a moment from a different perspective can reveal a new story.

For example, while visiting a local farmers' market, instead of taking a standard photo of the bustling crowd, focus on the details – a vendor's hands as they hand over fresh produce, the interplay of colors at a flower stall, or the steam rising from a cup of hot cider on a chilly morning. Rich in detail and emotion, these moments often make the most memorable photos.

## PHOTO SHARING WITH LOVED ONES

In the age of social media, sharing photos has become easier than ever. Yet, the plethora of platforms can be overwhelming. Consider creating a shared album on cloud services like *Google Photos* or *iCloud* for family and friends who appreciate regular updates. This way, you can upload photos to a single location where everyone has access without navigating multiple social media platforms. We like Google Photos because of its ease of sharing!

For more immediate sharing, pay attention to the simplicity of messaging apps. A quick snap sent through *WhatsApp* or *Telegram* can brighten someone's day without needing elaborate captions or hashtags. Remember, photography's joy lies in capturing and sharing moments, making distances feel less far away.

## CREATING DIGITAL ALBUMS

While letting photos live solely on our devices is tempting, creating digital albums can offer a more curated and accessible way to revisit memories. Many cloud services provide automated album creation(s) based on dates, locations, or events, but creating your albums allows for a personal touch. *Snapfish* and *Shutterfly* are popular apps to try. You can categorize them into vacations, family gatherings, or even simple joys like "Summer Sunsets" or "Winter Wonders."

This curation process can be a delightful trip down memory lane in itself. Set aside time every few months to sort through recent photos, selecting those that spark joy or capture a meaningful story. This keeps your digital photo library organized and ensures that the moments that matter most are always within easy reach.

As we navigate through the chapters of our lives, our smartphones witness the fleeting moments that define our days. Each photo we take is a testament to our journey, a digital footprint in the sands of time, from the mundane to the extraordinary. With some knowledge and creativity, we can ensure these footprints are as vivid and meaningful as the moments they capture, ready to be revisited and cherished for years to come.

## 1.2  THE WORLD AT YOUR FINGERTIPS: EXPLORING TRAVEL APPS

Exploring new places, tasting different cuisines, and immersing oneself in the culture of a foreign land is the stuff of dreams for many. Luckily, in our digital age, travel planning has evolved from a cumbersome task into an exciting prelude to the adventure itself, courtesy of many travel apps designed to make the process as smooth as a well-packed suitcase.

## TOP TRAVEL APPS FOR PLANNING

When piecing together your next getaway, a few taps on your smartphone can set you on the right path. Apps like *TripAdvisor* and *Lonely Planet* have become the go-to digital companions for travelers worldwide, offering a wealth of information on itineraries, flights, accommodations, and local attractions. These platforms provide user reviews and allow you to book your stay and experiences directly through the app, making travel planning an enjoyable breeze rather than a daunting task.

For those who love having their plans neatly organized, *TripIt* stands out by consolidating your travel information into a single, streamlined itinerary. Simply forward your booking confirmation emails to the app, and voila, you will have a detailed schedule complete with flight times, hotel addresses, and even weather forecasts.

## LOCAL EXPLORATION TOOLS

Once you've landed and are ready to explore, embracing the role of a temporary local rather than a tourist can transform your experience. Apps like *Yelp* and *Zomato* have become invaluable, guiding you to the best eateries in town, from the fanciest restaurants to the most unassuming street food stalls that only the locals know about. Meanwhile, apps such as *Culture Trip*, uncover hidden gems and cultural spots that might not make it to the front page of a guidebook but are sure to make your trip memorable.

For those adventurous souls keen on off-the-beaten-path experiences, *Roadtrippers* and *AllTrails* reveal hiking paths, scenic drives, and unique landmarks that aren't part of the typical tourist itinerary. These tools enrich your travel experience and foster a sense of discovery and adventure that stays with you long after you return home.

## STAYING SAFE WHILE TRAVELING

The excitement of travel also comes with ensuring one's safety, especially in unfamiliar territories. Apps like *Sitata* or the travel.state.gov website inform you about potential health risks, environmental hazards, and political unrest in your destination. Should you need immediate assistance, *TripWhistle Global SOS* provides emergency phone numbers for every country and geolocation capability to share your exact coordinates with first responders.

For those venturing into remote or less-traveled paths, offline maps and navigation tools such as *Google Maps*. You become indispensable, offering detailed, downloadable maps that don't require an internet connection. These resources keep you on track and provide peace of mind, knowing that help is always at hand should you need it.

## BUDGETING YOUR ADVENTURES

Dreaming of distant lands and exotic experiences often comes with the cold, hard reality of a budget. Thankfully, apps like *Trail Wallet* and *Mint* take the stress out of managing travel expenses, allowing you to focus more on the experiences and less on the costs. These apps enable you to set daily budgets, categorize your spending, and track your expenses in real-time, ensuring you can enjoy your adventure without financial worries looming over your head. Just remember: bring extra cash for that unplanned excursion or buy unique gifts for people back home.

*Skyscanner* and *Hopper* take the guesswork out of booking flights, alerting you to the best times to buy tickets and offering insights into flight price trends. Their predictive algorithms save you a pretty penny, which could be better spent on experiences rather than airfare. If you have an elaborate trip that includes multiple destinations or that is not planned through a vacation outfit, it might make sense to use a travel agency.

Similarly, apps dedicated to finding discounts on accommodations and activities can stretch your budget further. ***Booking.com*** and ***Airbnb*** often feature last-minute deals and unique stays that offer more bang for your buck, while ***Groupon*** and ***LivingSocial*** can lead you to discounted tickets for attractions, tours, and even spa days.

Navigating the world with these digital tools doesn't just simplify travel planning; it enriches the entire experience, allowing you to dive deeper into the essence of your destinations. With your smartphone as your guide, you're no longer just passing Through; you're engaging, discovering, and connecting with the world in a once unimaginable way. Whether finding that perfect sunset spot or a hidden culinary treasure or ensuring your journey is as smooth as it is enriching, these apps are your passport to a world of possibilities, effortlessly unfolding the globe at your fingertips.

## 1.3  STAY IN THE LOOP: SOCIAL MEDIA FOR BEGINNERS

Navigating the vast sea of social media platforms can sometimes feel like trying to choose the best ice cream flavor at a parlor that offers a hundred choices – overwhelming but exciting. For retirees or those about to step into this vibrant phase of life, social media isn't just about staying updated; it's a gateway to staying connected, learning new things, and sharing the joys of everyday life with others, near or far.

## CHOOSING THE RIGHT PLATFORMS

When selecting your digital hangout spots, think of it as finding the right community clubs to join – you want to go where your interests align and feel most at home. With widespread usage across generations, ***Facebook*** is a fantastic starting point for those looking to catch up with family and friends, share photos, and join groups with shared interests, from gardening to genealogy.

On the other hand, ***Instagram*** is your go-to for a more visual experience. It is perfect for sharing smartphone photography masterpieces or following content that inspires, be it travel, art, or cooking. Our teenage grandkids use instagram to post their recent photos, and we love seeing those!

For quick thinkers who love to stay abreast of the latest news or concisely share thoughts, ***Twitter*** offers an energetic platform to voice opinions and engage in lively discussions.

To find neighbors and friends with common interests: try ***Nextdoor*** for your neighborhood, and ***Meetup*** for local gatherings, concerts and fun.

## SETTING UP YOUR PROFILES

Once you've picked your platforms, setting up your profiles is like decorating your front porch – a balance between showcasing your personality and ensuring privacy. Start with a profile picture that reflects you or your interests; it could be a recent photo, a picture of your pet, or your favorite landscape shot. Then, fill in your bio with a sprinkle of humor or a dash of creativity, giving visitors a glimpse of who you are.

Privacy settings, however, are where you want to pay close attention. Take the time to go through each platform's privacy options, adjusting who can see your posts, send you friend requests, or tag you in photos. Think of it as setting the boundaries of your digital home, where you decide who comes knocking and who gets to peek through the windows.

## ENGAGING WITH CONTENT

With your digital home set up, it's time to engage. But remember, social media is not just about broadcasting your life; it's a two-way street. Start by following friends, family, and pages or groups that interest you. From there, liking, commenting, and sharing content keeps you active and strengthens your connections. It's like attending a social gathering and mingling – you listen, share stories, and respond to others, enriching your social experience.

Posting your content is equally important. Whether it's photos from a recent adventure, a recipe you mastered, or simply thoughts on a book you read, sharing adds to the tapestry of stories that make up social media. Don't shy away from using descriptive hashtags (e.g., #paris, #familylove) on platforms like Instagram or Twitter – think of them as signposts that guide others with similar interests to your content.

## MAINTAINING ONLINE SAFETY

First and foremost, be sure you have good anti-viral software such as *Norton Antivirus* or *McAfee*. While the digital world opens up new avenues for connection and exploration, it also necessitates a degree of caution. Start with a robust and unique password for each social media account, and consider enabling two-factor authentication where available, adding an extra layer of security. Be wary of friend requests from unknown individuals and think twice before clicking on links, even if they appear to come from friends – phishing attempts can sometimes disguise themselves well.

When sharing information, a good rule of thumb is never to post anything you wouldn't want publicly known – this includes addresses, phone numbers, or anything too personal. Additionally, regularly reviewing your friend lists and the apps connected to your social media accounts helps keep your digital space clean and secure.

In the end, with its myriad of platforms and possibilities, social media offers a unique opportunity to stay looped into the pulse of the world around us. From reconnecting with long-lost friends to discovering communities that share your passions, the digital age promises continued growth, learning, and connection. With a mindful approach to choosing platforms, setting up profiles, engaging with content, and maintaining online safety, the world of social media opens up a vibrant space for exploration and expression, enriching the retirement experience in ways once unimaginable.

## 1.4  LIFELONG LEARNING: EDUCATIONAL APPS FOR CURIOUS MINDS

The golden years are ripe for exploration, not just off the world around us but of the landscapes of knowledge and creativity that lie within. The beauty of living in the digital age is that learning new subjects, whether the mysteries of ancient history or the latest advancements in science, is as easy as tapping on a screen.

What did you enjoy when you were younger? Something that you wish you had studied? Now's the time! I wish I had taken Spanish because it is one of the universal languages, and I will learn Spanish with the apps available. Educational apps have turned smartphones and tablets into portable universities, offering lessons on virtually any topic you can dream of.

## FINDING APPS THAT MATCH YOUR INTERESTS

The first step to feeding your curiosity is pinpointing your interests. Do planets and galaxies far beyond our own ignite your imagination? You may have an affinity for classical music and be eager to learn more about the life and works of Beethoven and Mozart. There's an app for nearly every interest under the sun. For history buffs, apps like *The History Channel app* offer a ton of documentaries, articles, and historical tidbits. For science enthusiasts, the *NASA app* provides a gateway to the latest space missions, stunning universe images, and an array of educational videos.

Navigating through the app store, you'll find specialized apps tailored to niche interests. Plenty of resources exist, from bird watching and gardening to philosophy and literature. Start by exploring the 'Education' category in your app store, and don't hesitate to use the search function to narrow down your options. Reading reviews and ratings can also help you choose apps that have proven beneficial and engaging to others.

## STAYING MENTALLY ACTIVE

You've heard or read about the importance of keeping your brain agile as you age to prevent Alzheimer's and to be a more interesting conversationalist. Keeping the brain in shape is as important as physical fitness, especially as we age. Brain-training apps are designed with this goal, offering games and puzzles that challenge memory, problem-solving skills, and cognitive agility. Apps like *Lumosity* and *Peak* are leaders in this field, providing a variety of brain teasers and mental challenges developed by neuroscientists. These apps track your progress over time, offering insights into your strengths and areas for improvement.

Incorporating these brain exercises into your daily routine can be fun and rewarding. Set aside a few minutes each day for a mental workout, perhaps with your morning coffee or as a way to unwind in the evening. It's a habit that pays dividends, keeping your mind sharp and ready to tackle any new learning venture with enthusiasm.

## EXPLORING ONLINE COURSES

For those eager to drill down into a subject, online courses offer structured learning paths that range from introductory to advanced levels. Platforms like *Coursera* and *edX* bring courses from top universities around the globe right to your fingertips. Whether you're interested in psychology, computer science, art history, or anything in between, these platforms offer courses complete with video lectures, readings, and even assignments and exams to test your understanding. *LinkedIn learning* suits technology, management, and marketing skills if you continue to work or consult in your field.

Many of these courses are free, allowing you to audit the content at no cost. For a fee, you can also opt to receive a certificate upon completion, a tangible acknowledgment of your dedication and hard work. The flexibility of online courses means you can learn at your own pace, making it easy to fit new learning into a busy schedule or more leisurely retirement lifestyle. Alternatively, you can try *MasterClass:* for a moderate subscription fee, you'll have access to dozens of classes by world-renowned experts in various fields, such as writing, cooking, music, sports, and more.

## INTERACTIVE LEARNING TOOLS

Interactive tools bring subjects to life and make learning more enjoyable. Language learning apps like *Duolingo* and *Babbel* make mastering a new language engaging, using games and interactive exercises that improve your reading, writing, speaking, and listening skills. Moreover, these apps often include community features, allowing you to practice with native speakers and fellow learners, adding a social dimension to your study.

For a more immersive experience, virtual museum tours offer a window into the world's most famous museums, galleries, and historical sites. *Google Arts & Culture*, for example, lets you explore artworks in extraordinary detail, tour historical landmarks, and discover cultural treasures from across the globe. It's like having a personal tour guide in your pocket, ready to take you on a journey through history and art whenever you wish.

Similarly, apps designed for learning musical instruments combine video lessons with interactive feedback tools. Simply place your device near your instrument, and the app listens to you play, offering feedback and guidance to improve your technique. Whether picking up a guitar for the first time or dusting off the piano keys after years, these apps make the learning process accessible and enjoyable.

In embracing these educational apps and interactive tools, pursuing knowledge becomes a daily adventure, enriching the mind and soul with every discovery. With the world of learning at your fingertips, the opportunities for growth and exploration are limitless.

## 1.5  SIMPLIFYING LIFE: ORGANIZATIONAL APPS FOR DAILY USE

In a world that seems to spin faster with each passing day, keeping track of the little details—grocery lists, health routines, or family gatherings—can feel like juggling eggs while riding a unicycle. It's a delicate balance that technology seeks to simplify with a suite of apps designed to bring order to the chaos of daily life. Through the magic of these digital helpers, tasks that once cluttered our minds and counters find a neat and orderly place in our smartphones, freeing us to focus more on living and less on fretting over forgotten details.

## STREAMLINING  DAILY  TASKS

Imagine your smartphone as a Swiss Army knife for life's daily tasks. Apps like *Todoist* and *Any* transform your endless mental notes into manageable, actionable lists. With features that allow you to categorize tasks, set reminders, and even delegate chores to family members, these apps turn the daunting mountain of 'to-dos' into a series of easily navigable hills. For grocery shopping, apps like *Out of Milk* offer the convenience of sharing lists with family members, ensuring you never find yourself standing in the produce aisle wondering if someone else already picked up the tomatoes.

The beauty of these apps lies in their ability to remember you and their flexibility. They adapt to your life, whether you're planning a simple dinner, coordinating a multi-step project, or just trying to remember to water the plants. They serve as your digital secretary, quietly ensuring that nothing falls through the cracks.

## HEALTH AND WELLNESS TRACKERS

In pursuing a healthy lifestyle, keeping track of diets, exercise routines, and medication schedules can quickly become overwhelming. This is where health and wellness trackers act as your health coach tucked neatly in your pocket. Apps like *MyFitnessPal* and *Lose It!* make monitoring your diet as simple as scanning a barcode while providing a comprehensive nutritional information database. For those with specific fitness goals, apps like *Strava* and *Fitbit* track your physical activity, from daily steps to intense workouts, encouraging your journey towards better health.

Moreover, for individuals managing medications, *Medisafe* offers a solution to the often stressful medication management routine. Reminders for when to take pills, refill prescriptions, and even doctor's appointments alleviate one of the more critical stress points in health management. These trackers simplify healthcare logistics and empower you with information and support to maintain or improve your wellness.

## FINANCIAL MANAGEMENT

Money management, often a source of stress, can also benefit from the clarity and simplicity that apps provide. Budgeting apps like *Mint* and *YNAB (You Need A Budget)* demystify the world of finances, offering tools to track spending, set budgets, and even save for future goals. They connect with your bank accounts, categorizing each expense and showing you where your money is going—the necessary evils like bills or the occasional splurge on a fancy dinner out.

These apps do more than just track; they teach. They offer insights into spending habits and tips for further stretching your dollar. They transform financial management from a dreaded chore into an empowering activity, giving you control over your financial future.

## FAMILY COORDINATION

With families often running on schedules as complex as a CEO's, keeping everyone's plans in sync is paramount. *Cozi Family Organizer* or *Picnic* for family coordination, allowing you to consolidate appointments, school events, sports practices, and more into one shared calendar. Everyone in the family can add too and view this calendar, making missed appointments or double bookings a thing of the past.

But it goes beyond calendars. Shared shopping lists mean anyone can add items as needed, and a family journal offers a space to share photos and notes, keeping everyone in the loop on life's little moments and victories. It's like having a family meeting at your fingertips, ensuring everyone stays connected, no matter how divergent their paths may be on any given day. *Life360* is a family location tracking app that allows you to see the real-time location of family members and get alerts for safety and emergencies.

The digital age has brought us many gifts, but none so profound as the ability to simplify our lives, giving us back the time and mental space once consumed by the mundane. Through a selection of apps designed to streamline, inform, and connect, we find ourselves not just coping with the demands of daily life but thriving amidst them.

## LET'S BRIGHTEN THINGS UP WITH A TOUCH OF FUN!

Q: WHY DID THE RETIREE REFUSE TO USE A GPS?

A: BECAUSE THEY SAID, "IN MY DAY, WE FOUND OUR WAY BY SHEER 'SENIOR'ITY!"

# CHAPTER 2
# DIGITAL ENTERTAINMENT AND LEARNING MADE EASY

---

*"In the digital age, learning and entertainment are seamlessly integrated, offering boundless opportunities for growth and enjoyment."*

### DR. JANE MCGONIGAL, RENOWNED GAME DESIGNER AND AUTHOR

---

Picture this: You're sitting in your favorite armchair, a cup of tea in one hand, and an entire library at your fingertips. Gone are the days of musty bookshelves and late fees from forgotten returns. In our digital age, tablets have revolutionized media consumption and the essence of accessibility and convenience  in learning and entertainment. It's like having a personal librarian, cinema, and university rolled into one sleek device.

## 2.1  EBOOKS AND AUDIOBOOKS: BUILDING YOUR DIGITAL LIBRARY

### EMBRACING DIGITAL READING

The leap from paper to pixels is less about leaving behind the physical book and more about embracing the endless opportunities digital reading presents. With a tablet, you're no longer tethered to the weight of books. Instead, you carry a library that's as vast as your interests, ready to travel with you anywhere. Plus, with features like adjustable text size and built-in lighting, reading becomes accessible for everyone, turning strained eyes and bulky books into relics of the past.

### FINDING FREE AND DISCOUNTED EBOOKS

While building your digital library might sound like an expensive endeavor, it doesn't have to be. Numerous resources offer free or heavily discounted ebooks and audiobooks. Websites like *Project Gutenberg* and *LibriVox* are treasures of classics available for free download. For deals on more contemporary reads, *BookBub* and *Goodreads Deals* send personalized recommendations to your inbox, ensuring you never miss a sale on books you'll love. Libraries also offer digital loans through apps like *Libby* and **OverDrive,** making it easy to borrow the latest titles without stepping outside your home:

- **Project Gutenberg**: Over 60,000 free e-books, focusing on older works for which copyright has expired.
- **LibriVox**: Free public domain audiobooks read by volunteers from around the world.
- **BookBub**: Alerts on limited-time offers for free and discounted e-books across various genres.

## USING READING APPS

You'll need the right app to dive into your digital reading journey. *Kindle, Apple Books,* and *Google Play Books* are among the most user-friendly, offering extensive catalogs and features that enhance your reading experience. Here's what to look for in a reading app:

- **Adjustable Text Features**: Change the font size, style, and background color to suit your reading preferences.
- **Bookmarking and Note-Taking**: Easily mark important passages and jot down thoughts as you read.
- **Sync Across Devices**: Start reading on your tablet and pick up where you left off on your phone or computer.

## JOINING ONLINE BOOK CLUBS

One of the best parts of reading is sharing and discussing books. Online book clubs have flourished, providing communities for every genre and interest. From Facebook groups dedicated to mystery novels to Reddit's book communities discussing weekly reading selections, there's a space for every reader. These clubs offer a sense of belonging and expose you to books and perspectives you might not have encountered. Plus, participating in discussions can deepen your understanding and appreciation of the material, making reading a shared adventure.

Here are a few steps to get started with online book clubs:

- **Find Your Niche**: Search for groups based on your favorite genres or authors. Goodreads and Reddit are great places to start.
- **Engage**: Don't be shy! Share your thoughts on current reads, ask questions, and participate in discussions.
- **Recommend**: Got a book you love? Recommend it to the group. Sharing is part of the joy of being in a book club.

With their blend of technology and simplicity, tablets have opened the door to a world where reading is more accessible and engaging than ever before. Whether your exploring ancient texts available for free download or diving into the latest bestseller with a group of online friends, your digital library is a gateway to endless adventures, learning, and connection. With the right apps and resources, you're not just collecting books; you're curating experiences tailored to your interests and available at any moment's notice. So fill your digital shelves with worlds waiting to be discovered, all from the comfort of your armchair.

## 2.2   BRAIN GAMES: KEEPING SHARP WITH PUZZLE AND STRATEGY APPS

Brain games provide more than just fleeting entertainment; they're like a gym workout for your mind. Engaging regularly in puzzles and strategy-based challenges can significantly enhance cognitive functions, such as memory, attention, and problem-solving skills. It's a delightful method that allows you to sharpen your mental faculties while immersed in the joy of gameplay. Imagine turning the gears in your brain, not with strenuous effort, but through the fun and satisfaction of solving a puzzle or strategizing your next move in a game.

### BENEFITS OF BRAIN GAMES

Seeing how puzzle and strategy games act as catalysts for cognitive health is fascinating. They're not just digital pastimes but tools that stimulate brain activity, encouraging neural growth and new connections. Think about it – every time you solve a puzzle, you give your brain a mini workout, improving its ability to process information and solve problems. It's a process that, over time, can lead to sharper memory recall and a more attentive mind. Plus, there's the bonus of feeling a sense of accomplishment with each completed challenge, boosting your mood and motivation to tackle more.

## RECOMMENDED APPS FOR BRAIN TRAINING

Navigating the sea of available apps for brain training can be overwhelming, but there are a few standouts that consistently receive high praise for their effectiveness and enjoyability:

- *Peak:* Offers a broad range of games designed by neuroscientists to challenge memory, attention, problem-solving, and mental agility.
- *Elevate* Tailors training programs to your personal goals, improving math, reading, writing, and speaking skills.
- *CogniFit:* Measures and trains your cognitive skills, offering detailed feedback and recommendations for improvement.

Each of these apps presents a mixture of daily challenges and progress tracking, ensuring you're not just playing but growing. They manage to make the learning process engaging, turning complex cognitive exercises into fun and interactive games.

## SETTING UP A DAILY BRAIN WORKOUT ROUTINE

Integrating brain games into your daily routine is much like establishing any other healthy habit – it starts with setting aside a dedicated time. Morning can be an ideal time to wake up your brain and get it firing on all cylinders, but any time that fits your schedule will work. The key is consistency. Even just 15 minutes a day can lead to noticeable improvements over time. Here's a simple guide to get started:

- **Choose Your Apps**: Start with one or two apps that appeal to you. Overloading yourself with too many options might lead to decision fatigue.
- **Set a Daily Reminder**: Use your tablet or phone to set a daily alert, a friendly nudge to take a little time for your brain workout.

- **Track Your Progress**: Make it a habit to check your progress through the app's tracking features. It's motivating to see how far you've come.
- **Mix It Up**: Keep things fresh by varying the games or challenges you tackle. Most apps regularly update their offerings to keep you engaged.

## TRACKING YOUR BRAINS PROGRESS

One of the most rewarding aspects of using brain training apps is watching your progress unfold. These apps often have built-in tracking features that monitor your improvements across different cognitive areas. Watching your scores climb can be incredibly motivating as tangible evidence of your brain's growth and flexibility.

But progress in brain games isn't just about achieving high scores; it's about noticing changes in your daily life. You may find yourself remembering names more easily, mastering new skills more quickly, or solving everyday problems more efficiently. These real-world improvements are a true testament to the value of your daily brain workout routine.

The journey through puzzle and strategy apps involves discovery and improvement. It's about challenging yourself, not just within the confines of the game but in your everyday cognitive abilities. With each puzzle solved and strategy devised, you're not just passing the time; you're actively contributing to your cognitive health, keeping your mind sharp and ready to tackle whatever comes your way.

## 2.3   ART AND MUSIC: CREATIVE APPS FOR EXPRESSING YOUR INNER ARTIST

In a world where creativity knows no bounds, tablets offer a canvas and stage like no other. With the swipe of a finger or tap of a stylus, everyone from budding artists to seasoned musicians finds a digital playground teeming with possibilities. These modern marvels bring the art studio and concert hall to your living room, kitchen, or wherever you find your creative spark.

## EXPLORING DIGITAL ART PLATFORMS

For those who've ever dreamed of painting stunning landscapes or sketching their comic series but felt intimidated by the blank canvas, digital art platforms are your new best friends. Apps like *Procreate* and *Adobe Fresco* open up a world where mistakes are easily erased, and the undo button encourages experimentation without fear. These platforms are designed with both novices and pros in mind, offering an intuitive interface where your imagination can roam free.

- **Procreate**: Offers an extensive library of brushes and tools, making it perfect for everything from doodling to detailed illustrations.
- **Adobe Fresco**: Known for its live brushes that mimic watercolor and oil paints, bringing a traditional painting feel to the digital realm.

Starting with these apps can be a manageable investment in materials. Most offer basic versions for free, and with a stylus, your tablet transforms into a sketchbook that always has pages. For beginners, diving into digital art can start with simple tutorials available within these apps or through a wealth of online resources. Before you know it, you'll create works you're proud to call your own.

## MAKING MUSIC ANYWHERE

The joy of music creation isn't limited to those with a room full of instruments. Tablets bring the orchestra to you, offering apps that teach music theory, simulate instruments, and even guide you through composing your first song. Apps like *GarageBand* and *FL Studio Mobile* turn your tablet into a multi-instrument powerhouse where you can lay down tracks, mix, and produce songs that express your unique sound:

- **GarageBand**: A complete music creation studio right inside your tablet, it includes a variety of instruments and a full-featured recording studio.
- **FL Studio Mobile**: Offers high-quality synthesizers, drum kits, and a step sequencer for fast percussion programming.

Grasp the melody playing in your head, all with a few taps on the screen. These apps demystify the music products on a virtual piano, mix your first EDM process, and make it accessible to everyone. Whether you're learning chortrack or music creation, it has never been more within reach.

## SHARING YOUR CREATIONS

Art and music are not just about personal fulfillment; they're meant to be shared, sparking joy and inspiration in others. The digital age makes connecting with fellow creators and audiences more straightforward. Platforms like *Instagram* and *SoundCloud* serve as vibrant communities where artists and musicians showcase their work, gather feedback, and collaborate on new projects:

- **Instagram**: Ideal for visual artists; it's a place to share your artwork, connect with other artists, and discover new inspiration.
- **SoundCloud**: A music-focused platform that allows you to upload tracks, share them with a global audience, and connect with other musicians.

However, sharing is more comprehensive than on these platforms. Many art and music apps offer built-in sharing options, allowing you to publish your latest piece or track directly from the app to your social media profiles or personal websites. This seamless integration means your next masterpiece is just a few clicks away from reaching eyes and ears worldwide.

## LEARNING FROM MASTERS

While the journey of self-taught art and music creation is rewarding, there's something magical about learning from those who've mastered their craft. Apps like *MasterClass* and *Skillshare* directly bring lessons from renowned artists and musicians to your tablet. Imagine learning guitar techniques from Carlos Santana or exploring the creative process with celebrated illustrator Christoph Niemann:

- **MasterClass**: Offers courses taught by industry icons in arts, music, and more, combining high-quality video lessons with downloadable materials.
- **Skillshare**: Focuses on interactive learning with courses in drawing, painting, photography, and music production, encouraging you to practice as you learn.

These platforms provide expert guidance and insights into the creative journey, helping you refine your skills and find your artistic voice. With each lesson, you're not just learning techniques; you're being invited into a community of creators, all sharing the common goal of bringing beauty and expression into the world.

In this era where technology meets creativity, your tablet is the key to unlocking a universe where art and music flourish. From sketching your first digital portrait to composing a melody that echoes your heart's song, these apps are your companions on a voyage of artistic discovery. So let your inner artist out to play; with the world at your fingertips, who knows what wonders you'll create?

## 2.4   VIDEO CALLS: STAYING CONNECTED WITH FAMILY AND FRIENDS

In an age where distance feels like a mere concept rather than a barrier, video calling has seamlessly woven into our daily lives fabric. The bridge connects us to those who matter most, transforming miles into moments shared across screens. With many video call apps at our disposal, staying in touch has never been more dynamic or engaging.

## CHOOSING THE RIGHT VIDEO CALL APPS

Navigating the sea of video call applications can be as daunting as choosing the perfect coffee blend – options abound, but finding the one that suits your taste takes a bit of sampling. Apps like *Zoom* and *Skype* have long been staples for both personal and professional communications, prized for their reliability and wide range of features.

Then there's *FaceTime,* an exclusive club for Apple device enthusiasts, offering a sleek interface and seamless integration with your contacts. For those looking for something a bit more versatile, *Google Meet* provides an easy entry point, requiring only a Google account and an internet connection to get started. *WhatsApp* is another popular messaging app that works particularly well for free global video calls.

The choice boils down to compatibility with your device, the features you find most valuable, and, importantly, what your friends and family use. Ensure the app you choose supports group calls if you plan to host virtual family gatherings or friend meet-ups. Also, consider the ease of use, especially if you're helping less tech-savvy loved ones stay connected.

## SETTING UP GROUP CALLS

Organizing a video call that feels more like a get-together than a meeting is easier than you might think. Start by ensuring everyone you invite has access to the chosen app. Sending out clear instructions, perhaps even a quick guide on joining a call, can go a long way in making sure everyone's on the same page.

Once the technicalities are out, scheduling becomes your next focus. Apps like **Google Calendar** can be a great help, allowing you to set up an event and invite participants via email. They'll get a reminder before the call starts, ensuring no one misses out. When it's time, joining should be as simple as clicking a link.

## FUN WITH VIDEO CALLS

Who said video calls had to be all talk and no play? With features like virtual backgrounds and filters, each call becomes an opportunity for creativity and laughter. Imagine chatting from the beaches of Hawaii one day and the moon the next, all without leaving your living room. Apps like **Zoom** offer a range of fun backgrounds and effects and don't forget about **Snapchat** filters, which can be used through **Snap Camera** on various video call platforms.

Don't stop at backgrounds and filters, though. Games like charades or trivia can easily be adapted to video calls, making for a memorable night. Some apps even have built-in games or activities, perfect for when the conversation lulls.

## TROUBLESHOOTING COMMON ISSUES

Even the best-laid plans can encounter hiccups. Video calls are no exception, with issues ranging from unstable connections to audio glitches. Here are a few quick fixes for the most common problems:

- **Poor Connection**: Check your internet speed if the video or audio keeps cutting out. Moving closer to your Wi-Fi router or disconnecting other devices can improve the quality.
- **Audio Echoes**: This often happens when someone's microphone picks up audio from their speakers. Using headphones can eliminate this feedback loop.

- **Trouble Joining Calls**: Ensure the app is updated to the latest version. If someone can't find the invite, double-check the email address you sent it to.

Remember, patience and a bit of humor go a long way in smoothing over any technical snags. Sometimes, the best solution is to hang up and try reconnecting.

Video calls have truly transformed how we maintain relationships across distances, turning what once required travel and planning into moments easily captured through screens. Whether it's a quick check-in with a friend or a full-blown family reunion, the world of video calling apps ensures that no one feels too far away. With a bit of preparation and a willingness to embrace the quirks of technology, every call can be an adventure, a shared laugh, or a cherished connection, reminding us that though we may be apart, we're never truly alone.

## 2.5  COOKING AND NUTRITION: APPS FOR HEALTHY EATING

The digital age has transformed the kitchen into a hub of innovation and inspiration. With a tablet, you can access a global culinary world that guides your diet and cooking adventures toward healthier and more diverse horizons. Whether you're a seasoned chef or just starting to explore the wonders of cooking, a variety of apps can make the journey both simpler and more delightful.

## UNVEILING A WORLD OF RECIPES

Most of us will not be able to afford a personal chef in retirement. And take-out gets expensive. You're old tried and true recipes have seen better days, and you may be looking for more imaginative options. Imagine having a personal chef who understands your dietary needs and preferences and is ready to suggest many recipes at a moment's notice. That's precisely what recipe apps do. They offer many choices, from hearty vegan stews to gluten-free desserts, ensuring everyone at the table is catered to. Apps like *Yummly* and *Allrecipes* stand out for their extensive databases, user-friendly interfaces, and customization options. They allow you to filter recipes based on dietary restrictions, ingredients on hand, or the type of cuisine you're craving, turning meal planning into an exciting exploration of flavors. Here are two of my favorites:

- **Yummly**: Tailor's recipe suggestions based on dietary needs, dislikes, and allergy information.
- **Allrecipes**: Features a community of home cooks who rate, review, and offer recipe tweaks, adding a personal touch to your culinary ventures.

## STREAMLINING MEAL PLANNING AND GROCERY SHOPPING

Gone are the days of scribbled shopping lists and last-minute meal decisions. Meal planning apps integrate with your lifestyle, making organizing you're week's meals and shopping easy. With apps like *Mealime* and *Paprika*, creating a meal plan becomes straightforward, automatically generating shopping lists that ensure you never forget an ingredient again. These apps save you time and help reduce food waste by providing only what you need:

- *Mealime*: Creates personalized meal plans and shopping lists based on your food preferences and dietary goals.
- *Paprika:* Allows you to save recipes from anywhere on the web, plan meals, and make grocery lists, all in one place.

## TRACKING NUTRITIONAL INTAKE

Maintaining a balanced diet is crucial for health and well-being, yet understanding the nutritional content of your meals can be complex. Nutritional tracking apps demystify this process, offering insights into your daily intake of vitamins, minerals, and calories. Mentioned above, *MyFitnessPal* is a leader in this field, with a comprehensive database of foods and an easy-to-use barcode scanner for packaged goods. Such apps encourage mindful eating habits, allowing you to see the bigger picture of your diet and adjust as needed for optimal health.

## FOSTERING CONNECTIONS IN FOOD COMMUNITIES

Cooking is more than just a means to an end; it's an art form, a stress reliever, and, for many, a way to connect with others. Online cooking classes and forums offer a space to share this passion, learn new skills, and celebrate culinary successes with fellow food enthusiasts. Apps like *Tasty* and *MasterClass* provide access to cooking classes taught by renowned chefs. At the same time, forums like *Reddit* offer a place to exchange recipes, cooking tips, and food photography, enriching your culinary journey with the experiences and knowledge of a global community:

- *Tasty:* Known for its engaging, easy-to-follow recipe videos, it also offers interactive cooking classes.
- *MasterClass:* Features cooking classes taught by world-class chefs, offering insights into their techniques and culinary philosophies.

In wrapping up, the world of cooking and nutrition apps opens doors to a healthier, more informed, and connected culinary experience. From discovering new favorite dishes that meet your dietary needs to simplifying the meal planning process and gaining insights into your nutritional intake, these digital tools are invaluable in your quest for a balanced diet and culinary mastery. They not only make healthy eating more accessible but also transform cooking from a chore into an enjoyable adventure enriched by a community of fellow food lovers.

As we close this chapter, remember that each app, each recipe, and each meal is a step toward a more vibrant and healthful life. With the world's cuisines just a tap away, your kitchen has never been more alive. As we move forward, let's carry with us the flavors, the knowledge, and the connections we've gathered, ready to explore even more ways technology can enhance our daily lives. Now, let's turn the page and see what other digital marvels await.

## TIME FOR SOME LIGHTHEARTED AMUSEMENT:

Q: WHY DID THE SMARTPHONE GO TO SCHOOL?

A: BECAUSE IT WANTED TO IMPROVE ITS "CELL-F" ESTEEM AND HAVE SOME APP-SOLUTE FUN!

# CHAPTER 3
# EMBRACING MOTION, FUN EXERCISES FOR EVERYBODY

---

*"Physical fitness is not only one of the most important keys to a healthy body, it is the basis of dynamic and creative intellectual activity."*

**JOHN F. KENNEDY, 35TH PRESIDENT OF THE UNITED STATES**

---

Welcome to the chapter where motion takes center stage in the pursuit of well-being! Here, we embrace a diverse range of activities that cater to various fitness levels and preferences. Jump into the refreshing world of water aerobics, find your balance with Tai Chi, or enjoy the scenic beauty of nature walks.  Stretch and strengthen with yoga, and let loose with some lively dancing in your living room. We'll also introduce you to the exciting games of pickle ball and golf, where fun and fitness go hand in hand.

Get ready to move, groove, and elevate your health in enjoyable and dynamic ways. Let's get the ball rolling and embrace the joy of staying active.

## 3.1  GOLF: A SWING INTO RETIREMENT WITH SKILL, STRATEGY, AND SERENITY

Imagine a sport that blends the tranquility of nature with the excitement of a perfectly executed shot. This is golf—a game where every swing tests your precision and each hole presents a new challenge. Whether your approaching retirement or already enjoying your golden years, golf offers a journey through lush landscapes, promising personal achievements and friendly competition at every turn.

## BENEFITS OF GOLFING FOR PRE-RETIREES AND RETIREES

Golf is an excellent full-body workout for those nearing or in retirement. Walking the course provides great cardiovascular exercise, while swinging the club strengthens your arms, shoulders, and core. It's a sport that demands focus and strategy, serving as a mental workout that can reduce stress and improve concentration. The social aspect of golf is significant too, offering a chance to bond with friends or meet new people in a beautiful setting.

## GETTING STARTED WITH GOLF AT ANY STAGE

Your golf journey begins with finding a local course or driving range. Public courses are perfect for beginners, providing a relaxed environment to learn and practice. Equipment can be rented or bought second-hand initially. Taking a few lessons from a professional instructor can be invaluable to learn the basics and build a strong foundation. They'll offer personalized tips and help you navigate common mistakes, setting you on the path to a rewarding golf experience.

. . .

**Common Golf Exercises You Might Encounter:**

- **Driving**: Mastering your drive is essential for a solid start on each hole, focusing on both power and precision.
- **Putting:** The art of putting can significantly impact your game, requiring a careful balance of reading the green and gentle execution.
- **Chipping:** Perfecting the chip shot can save you strokes near the green, combining timing and technique for controlled shots.

Each round of golf offers a chance to hone these skills, with every course presenting its unique challenges. Golf's adaptability allows you to choose courses that match your skill level, enabling a gradual increase in difficulty as you improve.

## SOCIAL ASPECTS OF GOLF FOR PRE-RETIREES AND RETIREES

Golf is as much about camaraderie as it is about competition. Joining a golf club or league introduces you to a community of like-minded individuals, providing an opportunity to share experiences, learn from others, and celebrate achievements together. Tournaments or casual games add an element of fun, while post-round conversations at the clubhouse offer a space to relax and connect.

The golf course is a place where lasting friendships are formed, and memories are cherished. Whether sharing a laugh over a missed shot or congratulating a partner on a birdie, the relationships built on the green can be enduring. This sense of community is what makes golf more than just a game; it's a rewarding experience that enhances both your physical and social well-being as you transition into and enjoy retirement.

In summary, golf is an ideal sport for those approaching or in retirement, offering a unique combination of physical activity, mental stimulation, and social interaction. It invites you to enjoy the outdoors, challenge yourself, and connect with others. So, whether you're preparing for retirement or already there, consider taking up golf and join the millions who have found joy in this timeless game. The fairways await, and a new adventure is just beginning.

## 3.2  WATER AEROBICS: LOW-IMPACT EXERCISE FOR STRENGTH AND FLEXIBILITY

Picture a world where exercise doesn't mean heavy lifting at the gym or running marathons. Instead, imagine slipping into a pool, feeling the water's embrace, and starting a workout that feels more like a dance. That's the magic of water aerobics—a form of exercise that combines the joy of movement with the soothing properties of water.

### BENEFITS OF WATER RESISTANCE

With natural resistance, water turns basic movements into a strengthening workout, almost like magic. Imagine lifting weights, but you're pushing against water instead of dumbbells. This resistance is gentle yet effective, making muscles work harder without the strain on joints in a traditional gym setting. It's a game-changer for flexibility, too. Moving through water strengthens muscles and helps them stretch, improving flexibility. So, whether you're reaching down to tie a shoe or picking something off a top shelf, those movements become easier over time.

## GETTING STARTED WITH WATER AEROBICS

Finding a local class or a community pool offering water aerobics is your first step. Most community centers and gyms with pools have classes ranging from beginner to advanced. And don't forget the local YMCA - they have affordable memberships, clean facilities, and helpful staff. No special equipment is needed to start, just a swimsuit and a towel. Some classes suggest water shoes for extra grip on the pool floor, but they're optional on day one.

Here's a tip: Try a few classes to find the right fit. Instructors have different styles, and the right one can make all the difference. Also, remember to ask about the pool's depth and temperature. Warmer and shallower pools can be more comfortable, especially if you're just dipping your toes into water workouts. Water aerobics isn't just a single exercise; it's a variety of movements that target different parts of the body. Here are a few you might encounter:

- **Aqua Jogging**: It is excellent for cardiovascular health without impacting knees and hips like jogging but in water.
- **Leg Lifts**: Standing by the pool's edge for support, lifting your legs against the water's resistance. It's fantastic for strengthening leg and abdominal muscles.
- **Arm Curls**: Using water weights, performing arm curls works the biceps and triceps. Imagine doing bicep curls, but each pull is met with the gentle push of water.

Each class mixes and matches exercises, ensuring a full-body workout that always gets exciting. Plus, the beauty of water aerobics is its adaptability. Exercises can be modified to increase or decrease intensity, making them perfect for anyone, regardless of fitness level or age.

## SOCIAL ASPECTS OF WATER AEROBICS

The community is one of the best parts of joining a water aerobics class. It's not just about getting fit; it's about laughing, sharing stories, and encouraging each other. Picture this: everyone in the pool, moving to the beat of the music, cheering each other on. It's a workout that doesn't feel like work.

Many find lifelong friends in these classes. It's a place where social-izing and health go hand in hand. After a few sessions, you're part of a squad, not just attending a class. Celebrating birthdays, achievements, or just the fact that it's Wednesday becomes part of the routine. This sense of community is a powerful motivator, making you look forward to each class for the exercise and the joy of being part of something bigger.

Water aerobics is a testament to the fact that taking care of our bodies doesn't have to be a solitary journey or a chore. It celebrates what our bodies can do at any age with the proper support and environment. So, dive in. The water's fine, and the company's even better.

Discover Pickle Ball, the ideal sport for retirees looking to combine social interaction with physical activity. This game, a blend of tennis, badminton, and table tennis, offers a low-impact, high-fun way to stay active and engaged.

### 3.3 Pickleball: A Perfect Match for Retirees Seeking Fun and Fitness

Discover pickleball, the ideal sport for retirees looking to combine social interaction with physical activity. This game, a blend of tennis, badminton, and table tennis, offers a low-impact, high-fun way to stay active and engaged.

## BENEFITS OF PICKLEBALL

Pickleball is tailored for retirees, providing a gentle yet effective workout that enhances agility, balance, and coordination without putting undue stress on the joints. It's a mental workout too, keeping the mind sharp as players strategize and react quickly to the game's fast pace. Beyond the physical and mental benefits, pickle ball's true charm lies in its community. It's a social sport that brings people together, fostering friendships and a sense of belonging.

## GETTING STARTED WITH PICKLEBALL FOR RETIREES

Beginning your pickleball journey is straightforward and inexpensive. You'll need just a paddle and a ball, and you can find courts at local recreational centers or parks, often with special times reserved for senior players. Starting with the basics, retirees can learn through clinics, classes, or online resources tailored to their pace. As skills develop, joining a pickle ball group or club can provide structured play and social opportunities, enhancing the experience.

**Here are some Pickleball exercises suitable for retirees:**

- **Dinking**: A gentle, controlled shot ideal for those wanting to avoid high-impact movements, focusing on precision rather than power.
- **Volleying**: Engage in light, quick exchanges at the net to maintain reflexes and hand-eye coordination without strenuous movements.
- **Serving**: An underhand serve that starts the game, allowing for a relaxed, consistent, and accurate play.

Pickleball is adaptable, with exercises and gameplay that can be modified to suit varying fitness levels, ensuring everyone can participate and enjoy the game.

**Social Aspects of Pickleball for Retirees**

The welcoming and inclusive community of pickleball stands out, especially for retirees. It's not just about playing; it's about connecting, sharing stories, and supporting one another. Group events, social gatherings, and tournaments add an extra layer of enjoyment, making pickle ball more than just a sport—it's a social lifeline.

Pickleball is a fantastic choice for retirees seeking a fun, social, and active lifestyle. It's a sport that celebrates what our bodies can do at any age, within a community that values connection and well-being. So, step onto the court and experience the joy and camaraderie that pickleball has to offer. The game is on, and the fun is just beginning!

## 3.4  TAI CHI: THE ART OF MOVEMENT FOR BALANCE AND SERENITY

Tai Chi, an ancient Chinese martial art known for its slow and deliberate movements, is like a dance where each posture flows into the next in a graceful and meditative sequence. Originating from self-defense techniques, its evolution into a moving meditation emphasizes internal strength, balance, and the flow of what's known as 'qi' or life energy. The beauty of Tai Chi lies in its simplicity and the profound impact on health, making it more than just physical exercise; it's a practice for the mind, body, and spirit.

Tai Chi is a welcoming practice that doesn't discriminate by age or fitness level. Its gentle nature makes it particularly appealing for retirees looking to stay active without the risks associated with high-impact exercises. The movements, while simple, are designed to build strength, improve balance and flexibility, and reduce stress, all of which are crucial for maintaining an active and fulfilling lifestyle as we age. For individuals with limitations or concerns about mobility, Tai Chi offers modifications and can be adapted to be performed while seated, ensuring that the benefits of the practice are accessible to all.

Finding a suitable Tai Chi class might initially seem daunting, but many communities offer classes designed for beginners or older adults. Start by checking local community centers, senior centers, or fitness clubs for classes. Many Tai Chi instructors also offer private sessions or small group classes, providing a more personalized introduction to the practice. Additionally, for those who prefer to start learning at home, a wealth of resources is available online, including instructional videos and apps dedicated to Tai Chi practice. When choosing a class or resource, look for certified instructors who have experience working with beginners and those with physical limitations to ensure a safe and rewarding learning experience.

One of the most compelling reasons to incorporate Tai Chi into your routine is its mental and emotional benefits. The practice is deeply rooted in mindfulness, encouraging practitioners to focus on their movements and breath, which helps quiet the mind and reduce stress. This meditative aspect of Tai Chi strengthens the mind-body connection, promoting inner peace and well-being. Regular practice has been shown to improve focus and mental clarity, reduce anxiety and depression, and even enhance sleep quality. These benefits, as well as physical ones, make Tai Chi a holistic practice, nurturing the body, mind, and spirit.

In essence, Tai Chi is more than just an exercise; it's a pathway to a more balanced and serene state of being. With each gentle movement, practitioners are invited to connect deeply with themselves, finding strength and tranquility in the flow of life's energies. Whether you're looking to improve your physical health, reduce stress, or simply find a moment of peace in your day, Tai Chi offers a gentle yet powerful practice that enriches life in profound ways.

## 3.4 YOGA: POSES AND PRACTICES FOR EVERY LEVEL

Yoga, an ancient practice that has endured and evolved through centuries, offers more than just a way to stretch and strengthen the body. It's a path towards achieving a balance of mind, body, and spirit, accessible to everyone, regardless of age or fitness level. The beauty of yoga lies in its flexibility—not just the physical kind but in how it can be adapted to meet the needs and capabilities of each practitioner.

## YOGA FOR HEALTH AND FLEXIBILITY

The benefits of incorporating yoga into your routine are manifold. Regular practice can significantly enhance flexibility, making everyday movements more accessible and fluid. But the advantages continue beyond there. Yoga also plays a crucial role in improving balance, preventing falls, and maintaining independence as we age. Moreover, the strength gained from various yoga poses contributes to overall well-being, supporting the body's core and improving posture:

- **Flexibility**: Gradual stretching through yoga poses increases the range of motion, easing the stiffness of age.
- **Balance**: Poses focusing on standing and stability can reduce the risk of falls, a common concern among older adults.
- **Strength**: Building muscle through low-impact yoga poses supports joint health and enhances daily functional movements.

## STARTING WITH YOGA

Finding a suitable class or resource for newcomers too yoga can be the first step toward a rewarding practice. It's crucial to begin at a level that matches your current abilities and to understand that yoga is a personal journey, with progress measured not by comparison with others but by personal growth and well-being:

- **Choosing a Class**: Look for beginner or gentle yoga classes focusing on foundational poses and breathing techniques. Many community centers, gyms, and yoga studios offer classes designed for newcomers or older adults.
- **Understanding Yoga Styles**: Familiarize yourself with the various styles of yoga, such as Hatha, which is generally slower-paced and focuses on basic postures, or Restorative, which uses props to support the body in relaxing deeply. Selecting a style that resonates with your personal goals and physical condition can enhance your yoga experience.
- **Practicing Safely**: Always listen to your body, avoiding any movements or poses that cause discomfort. Inform your instructor of any injuries or health conditions before class so they can offer modifications as needed.

## ADAPTABLE YOGA POSES

Yoga's adaptability is one of its most appealing aspects, allowing it to be accessible to everyone. Many poses can be modified to accommodate various levels of mobility and flexibility, ensuring that everyone can participate and benefit from the practice:

- **Chair Yoga**: Ideal for those with limited mobility, chair yoga modifies traditional poses for seated or standing support, making yoga accessible to those who cannot sit on the floor or stand for long periods.
- **Wall Yoga**: Using a wall for support can help with balance and alignment, making poses more accessible and safer for beginners or those with balance concerns.
- **Prop Use**: Bolsters, blocks, and straps can modify poses, bringing the ground 'closer' or aiding in the safe deepening of stretches, ensuring that each individual can experience the benefits of each pose without strain.

## THE MIND-BODY CONNECTION

At the heart of yoga is the connection between mind and body, achieved through focused breathing and mindfulness. This aspect of yoga offers profound mental health benefits, from reducing stress and anxiety to enhancing mood and cognitive function.

- **Breath Work**: Yoga teaches controlled breathing techniques to calm the nervous system, reduce stress, and improve focus and concentration.
- **Mindfulness**: By bringing attention to the present moment and the body's sensations, yoga fosters mindfulness, reducing stress and increasing emotional well-being.
- **Meditation**: Many yoga classes incorporate guided imagery or silent reflection to create a state of deep relaxation and mental clarity.

Yoga offers a holistic approach to health and well-being, integrating physical exercise with mental and spiritual practices that can enrich the quality of life. Its adaptability and focus on the individual make it a suitable and beneficial practice for people at any stage of life, providing a valuable tool for navigating the challenges of aging with grace and vitality. Through regular practice, yoga can offer a pathway to improved physical health, mental clarity, and a more profound sense of peace and contentment. Other physical activities, such as Qi Gong or Pilates, have similar benefits.

## 3.5  NATURE WALKS: EXPLORING LOCAL PARKS AND TRAILS

Stepping outside, the world offers an open invitation to wander, to breathe deeply, and to connect with the earth underfoot and the sky overhead. Nature walks, a simple yet profound activity, open avenues to enhance physical well-being and nourish the soul. Walking amidst trees, along riversides, or across open fields, you're not just moving your body but immersing yourself in the tranquility and beauty of the natural world.

## THE JOY OF NATURE WALKS

Venturing out on a nature walk, even if it's just a short stroll in a nearby park, can be a transformative experience. Walking in nature has lowered stress levels, improved mood, and increased happiness. It's the perfect antidote to the hustle and bustle of daily life, offering a space for quiet reflection and a break from screens and concrete. Whether it's the rustling of leaves, the chirping of birds, or the gentle flow of a stream, nature's symphony has a way of soothing the mind and invigorating the body.

## CHOOSING THE RIGHT TRAILS

Finding trails that suit your level of fitness and mobility ensures that your nature walk is enjoyable and safe. Here are some tips for selecting the right path:

- **Research Ahead**: Websites and apps dedicated to outdoor activities often provide detailed information on trails, including difficulty levels, length, and elevation change. Look for trails marked as "easy" or "accessible" if you're starting or have mobility concerns.
- **Consult Local Resources**: Visitor centers, park offices, and community boards can be gold mines of information on local walking paths. They can offer up-to-date advice on trails best suited to your needs.
- **Start Small**: If you're new to nature walks, begin with shorter trails that don't require significant elevation changes. As you build your confidence and stamina, gradually increase the distance and complexity of your walks.
- Apps like *AllTrails* and *TrailLink* help you to find and scope out local trails based on geography and difficulty. Or try

*Komott* or *REI Co-op* Guide to National Parks to find good trails and points of interest.

## SAFETY AND PREPARATION

Before you lace up your walking shoes, a bit of preparation can go a long way in making your nature walk both safe and enjoyable:

- **Dress Appropriately**: Wear comfortable, weather-appropriate clothing and sturdy walking shoes. Layers are your friend, allowing you to adjust to changes in temperature.
- **Pack Essentials**: A small backpack with water, snacks, sunscreen, and a basic first-aid kit can address basic needs and mishaps.
- **Inform Someone**: Always let someone know where you're going and when you expect to return, especially if you're venturing into less populated areas.
- **Check the Weather**: A quick look at the weather forecast can help avoid getting caught in rain or extreme heat, ensuring a more pleasant walk.
- **Applications:** Apps like Life360 or FindMy allow family members to track each other for rendezvous and safety.

## ENGAGING WITH NATURE

To elevate your nature walk from a simple physical activity to a richer experience, try incorporating elements that engage your senses and curiosity:

- **Bird Watching**: Bring binoculars and a bird guidebook or app. Identifying different species can add an element of discovery and connection to your walk.
- **Photography**: Capture the beauty of the landscape, intriguing plants, or wildlife you encounter. Photography encourages you to observe your surroundings more closely and to appreciate

the small details.

- **Citizen Science Projects**: Participate in projects that allow you to collect data on wildlife, plant species, or environmental conditions. Apps like iNaturalist connect you with scientists and other nature enthusiasts, contributing to conservation efforts and research.
- **Mindful Walking**: Practice mindfulness by focusing on your breath, the feel of the ground under your feet, and the sounds and smells around you. This can deepen your connection to nature and enhance the mental health benefits of your walk.

Nature walks offer a simple yet profound way to connect with the natural world, promoting physical health, mental well-being, and a deeper appreciation for the environment. With some preparation and a spirit of curiosity, each walk can become an adventure, a moment of peace, and a step towards a more balanced and joyful life.

## 3.6   DANCING AT HOME: FUN ROUTINES TO KEEP YOU MOVING

Dancing, often seen as the heartbeat of joyous celebrations, carries many perks extending far beyond the dance floor. This rhythmic movement is a form of expression and a comprehensive workout that boosts heart health and uplifts your mood. Imagine the endorphins, those feel-good hormones, flooding your system as you sway and twirl to your favorite tunes, transforming your living room into a haven of happiness and vitality.

## THE BENEFITS OF DANCING

The allure of dancing lies in its dual impact on physical and emotional well-being. On one hand, it's a cardiovascular activity that gets your heart pumping, akin to jogging or cycling, but with rhythm and soul. It's a fun way to improve stamina, tone muscles, and enhance coordination and balance—all critical for staying agile as years go by. On the other hand, dancing lifts spirits, alleviates stress, and foster an overall sense of well-being. This fusion of joy and health makes dancing an unparalleled activity for people of all ages.

## FINDING YOUR RHYTHM

Diving into dancing is as simple as letting the music guide you, but a bit of structure can turn random moves into a fulfilling routine. Here's how to get started:

- **Select a Dance Style**: From the elegance of ballroom to the energetic beats of hip-hop, there's a dance style for every taste. Begin with what moves you—literally and figuratively.
- **Online Tutorials and Classes**: Platforms like *YouTube* offer a number of dance tutorials, offering step-by-step guidance for beginners. Subscription services and apps dedicated to dance instruction provide structured lessons for those seeking more in-depth exploration.
- **Creating a Safe Space**: Ensure your dance area is clear of obstacles. A smooth, non-slip floor and comfortable footwear (or barefoot, depending on the style) can prevent mishaps, making your dance sessions carefree and safe.

## DANCE PARTIES FOR ONE OR MORE

Who says you need a crowd to have a party? A solo dance session can be incredibly liberating, a time to let loose without self-consciousness. Yet, inviting friends or family members to join via video call can turn it into a delightful social event. Here are some ideas to make your dance parties memorable:

- **Theme Nights**: Choose themes for your dance sessions—'80s night, Latin groove, or pop divas—to keep things exciting. Dressing the part adds to the fun!

- **Playlists**: Collaborate on a playlist, allowing everyone to contribute their favorite dance tracks. It's a great way to discover new music and ensure something for everyone.
- **Virtual Dance-Offs**: Add a competitive edge with friendly dance-offs. Take turns showcasing moves or choreographies, then vote on the most creative or energetic performance.

## ADAPTING DANCE MOVEMENTS

Embracing dance means recognizing and honoring your body's capabilities and limits. Here's how to ensure that dancing remains inclusive and enjoyable for everyone:

- **Listen to Your Body**: Pay attention to how your body feels during and after dancing. If certain moves cause discomfort, try adjusting them or choose better alternatives.
- **Use Props and Support**: Chairs or walls can support balance during dance moves, making them accessible to those with mobility concerns.
- **Modify Movements**: Many dance steps can be modified to be less strenuous. More minor, controlled movements offer a way to participate without strain, ensuring that the joy of dancing is available to all, regardless of fitness level or physical ability.

**Let's inject some playfulness:**

---

Q: WHY DID THE RETIREE START DOING YOGA?

A: BECAUSE HE HEARD IT WOULD HELP HIM FIND HIS "INNER PIECE" OF CAKE!

---

# CHAPTER 4
# DISCOVERING THE GREAT JOY IN MOTHER NATURE

*"In every walk with nature, one receives far more than he seeks."*

### JOHN MUIR

This chapter isn't just about going outside; it's about reconnecting with the world around us in a way that enriches our lives and brings us closer to the planet's heartbeat. Regardless of your retirement plans, I hope you will make time for nature's adventure.

## 4.1 GETTING STARTED WITH BIRD WATCHING

Imagine stepping into your backyard, local park, or any slice of greenery you can find and realizing it's not just a space. It's a live stage where nature unfolds its tales day by day. Here, the actors are the birds, each species playing its unique role in the ecosystem and delighting us with their presence.

Bird watching, or birding as it's fondly known among enthusiasts, stands out as an activity that effortlessly blends the joy of discovery with the serenity of being in nature. It's a pursuit that requires just a bit of curiosity, patience, and an openness to see the world through a new lens.

Bird watching is like opening the door to a new dimension where time slows down, and the focus sharpens on the flutter among the leaves or the distant call from a treetop. Here's how to start:

- **Binoculars**: Your primary tool. Opt for a pair that's not too heavy with a magnification of 8x or 10x, striking a balance between a wide field of view and detailed observation.
- **Field Guide**: A book or app that helps identify birds. Look for one with clear illustrations or photos, range maps, and descriptions of songs and behaviors.
- **Notebook**: For jotting down what you see, a simple notebook or a birding app where you can record sightings, locations, and notes about behavior or appearances.

## BIRD WATCHING AS A GATEWAY TO NATURE

Birding encourages you to look closer at the environment. It's not just about the birds but also where they live, what they eat, and how they interact with the world around them. This deeper understanding fosters a greater appreciation for local ecosystems and the importance of conservation. Suddenly, a walk in the park becomes a mini-safari, where you're looking for who's visiting the feeders today or which migratory guests have stopped by.

## JOINING A BIRD-WATCHING GROUP

While birding can be a peaceful solo activity, joining a group adds a social layer to the experience. Groups offer shared knowledge, tips on the best local spots, and the joy of celebrating rare sightings together. Finding a group can be as simple as checking social media for local birding clubs or visiting a nearby nature center. Many groups host regular walks, which can be especially helpful for beginners looking to learn from more experienced birders.

## BENEFITS FOR MIND AND BODY

Bird-watching can be surprisingly meditative. Focusing on the search for birds can quiet the mind, while the excitement of spotting a new species provides a burst of joy. The benefits also extend to the physical, encouraging you to spend more time outdoors, walking, and exploring different terrains. It's an activity that perfectly balances gentle physical exercise and mental relaxation, offering a unique way to unwind and recharge.

In wrapping up, bird watching emerges as a simple yet profoundly enriching way to connect with the natural world. It invites us to slow down, observe, and appreciate the incredible diversity of life outside our doors. With each bird spotted and identified, we're reminded of the beauty and complexity of nature and our responsibility to protect it. So grab those binoculars, open your field guide, and step into the great outdoors, where a world of discovery awaits.

## 4.2  FISHING: RELAXING BY THE WATER'S EDGE

Fishing is a pastime that can whisk you away from the daily grind, offering moments of peace and reflection by the water's edge. It's a hobby that doesn't call for youth or strength but rather patience, a bit of know-how, and an appreciation for the outdoors. Whether casting a line from a riverbank or sitting by a serene lake, fishing is about more than the catch – it's about embracing the tranquility of nature and the thrill of the wait.

## INTRODUCTION TO FISHING

Understanding the basics sets the stage for rewarding experiences for those new to the sport. Several fishing methods are suited to different environments and targets:

- **Fly Fishing**: Utilizing artificial flies to mimic insects or baitfish, perfect for freshwater rivers and streams.
- **Spinning** is a versatile technique where lures or baits are cast and retrieved, and it is suitable for fresh and saltwater.
- **Still Fishing**: The classic method of baiting a hook, casting it out, and waiting for a bite is ideal for beginners.

The essential gear you'll need includes a fishing rod and reel, suitable lines, hooks, and bait or lures, depending on your chosen method. A comfortable chair, a hat for shade, and a good sunscreen round out the basics, ensuring you're prepared for a day by the water.

## THE THERAPEUTIC EFFECTS OF FISHING

The calm that comes from being near water, the focus required to bait a hook, and the anticipation of a bite combine to create a meditative experience. Fishing invites you to disconnect from the digital world and tune into the natural rhythm of the water and its inhabitants. This immersion in nature can significantly melt away stress, offering a peaceful escape that rejuvenates the mind and spirit. Studies suggest that time spent in such activities can lower blood pressure, reduce anxiety, and improve concentration, underscoring the mental health benefits of fishing.

## ACCESSIBLE FISHING SPOTS

Finding the right spot to fish is key to a successful outing. Many parks, lakes, and rivers offer designated fishing areas with amenities like accessible docks, clear signage, and even tackle loaner programs for those without gear. Here's how to find them:

- **Local Wildlife Agencies**: Websites and offices often list fishing sites, including details on accessibility and species you're likely to catch.
- **Fishing Apps and Websites**: Resources like *Fishbrain* provide user-shared information on spots, catches, and conditions.
- **Ask Around**: Local bait shops and fishing clubs are wells of information, offering insights into the best times to go and the spots welcoming to all.

When selecting a spot, consider ease of access, especially if mobility is a concern. Many places now feature paved paths to the water and platforms designed for wheelchair users, ensuring everyone can enjoy the sport.

## CATCH AND RELEASE ETHICS

As the sport of fishing continues to evolve, so does our understanding of its impact on aquatic ecosystems. Practicing catch and release is one way to enjoy fishing while contributing to conservation efforts. Here are a few pointers to ensure it's done responsibly:

- **Use the Right Tackle**: Barbless hooks and soft lures minimize injury to the fish, making a successful release more likely.
- **Handle with Care**: Wet your hands before handling the fish to protect its slime coat. Hold it gently, avoiding contact with its gills and eyes.

- **Quick Release**: Keep the fish in the water as much as possible, and use a hook remover for a swift release.

This mindful approach helps maintain fish populations and ensures future generations can enjoy the thrill of fishing just as we do. It's a small way to give back to the waters that offer us so much relaxation and joy whether the fish decides to bite.

## 4.3 GARDENING: GROWING YOUR OWN FLOWERS AND VEGETABLES

Digging into the earth, planting seeds, and watching life sprout and flourish under your care—gardening is a pastime that reconnects us with the cycles of nature. It's both a craft and a delight, offering a unique blend of physical activity, mental engagement, and emotional fulfillment. From the vibrant colors of flowers to the crisp freshness of home-grown vegetables, gardening celebrates life's simple pleasures.

## THE RICH REWARDS OF CULTIVATING YOUR GARDEN

Gardening goes beyond beautifying your space; it invests in your health and happiness. Gardening is a moderate exercise that can improve endurance, strength, and flexibility. Bending to plant, stretching to reach, and walking back and forth with a watering can are physical activities that contribute to a healthier body.

But the benefits of gardening aren't just physical. The garden is a canvas for creativity, where you can express yourself through the design and selection of plants and the care you put into nurturing them. Watching your garden grow can also be incredibly rewarding, offering a sense of accomplishment and pride. Moreover, gardens are sanctuaries of tranquility and beauty, spaces where you can relax, unwind, and find peace amidst the greenery and blooms.

## PLANTING THE SEEDS OF YOUR GARDEN HAVEN

Starting a garden is an adventure that begins with envisioning what you want to create, be it a vegetable patch, a bed of blooming flowers, or a mix of both. Here's how to get started:

- **Choose Your Site**: Look for a spot with adequate sunlight, as most vegetables and flowers thrive in bright light. Ensure the area has good drainage and access to water.
- **Prepare the Soil**: Test the soil to see what nutrients it may need. Adding compost can improve soil health, providing a rich plant foundation.
- **Select Your Plants**: Consider your climate and the amount of sun and rain your garden will get. Pick plants that will thrive in your conditions for the best results.
- **Plan Your Layout**: Arrange taller plants in the back and shorter ones in the front for a visually pleasing setup. Remember to space your plants according to their mature size, allowing room for growth.

Whether working with a vast backyard or a modest balcony space, gardening is adaptable. Container gardening, for instance, is perfect for small spaces, allowing you to grow herbs, flowers, and even some vegetables in pots.

## MAKING GARDENING ACCESSIBLE FOR EVERYONE

Not everyone can kneel in the dirt or wield a heavy shovel, but that shouldn't keep anyone from experiencing the joy of gardening. Here are a few adaptations that make gardening more accessible:

- **Raised Beds and Container Gardening**: Elevating your garden to waist height means less bending and easier access. Containers can be placed on tables or wheeled stands for mobility.
- **Ergonomic Tools**: Lightweight tools with easy-grip handles reduce strain on hands and wrists, making gardening tasks more comfortable.
- **Drip Irrigation Systems**: Installing a simple drip irrigation system with a hose or watering can eliminate the need for daily watering, saving time and effort.

These adaptations ensure that gardening remains a source of joy and fulfillment, regardless of physical limitations.

## CULTIVATING MORE THAN PLANTS

Gardening is rarely a solitary pursuit. It is a beautiful way of bringing people together, whether through exchanging plants and produce or the shared experiences in community gardens. Here's how you can connect with others through gardening:

- **Join a Community Garden**: Community gardens offer space to grow your plants and provide camaraderie as you work alongside neighbors and fellow garden enthusiasts.
- **Participate in Gardening Clubs or Online Forums**: These groups are fantastic for sharing tips, seeking advice, and celebrating successes. They can also be a source of cuttings, seeds, and plants.
- **Volunteer**: Many schools, hospitals, and community centers have gardens that benefit from volunteers. It's a rewarding way to share your love of gardening while helping others.

In every seed planted and every flower nurtured, gardening unfolds as a testament to the beauty and resilience of life. It teaches patience, care, and the reward of tending to the growth of something outside

oneself. Through gardening, we cultivate plants and a deeper connection to the earth and each other, enriching our lives in countless,
unforeseen ways.

## 4.4   SCENIC DRIVES: DISCOVERING THE BEAUTY BEYOND YOUR DOORSTEP

Ah, the open road—a canvas of landscapes waiting to be explored,
each turn revealing a new vista that paints itself into the tapestry of our
memories. Scenic drives offer a unique way to experience the grandeur
of the outdoors from the comfort of our vehicles. It's about the wind in
your hair, the sun on your face, and the world spread out before you, a
reminder that beauty lies just beyond the threshold of our everyday
lives.

## MAPPING OUT YOUR ADVENTURE

Before you set off, some preparation can turn a simple drive into an
unforgettable journey. Start with selecting your route. The internet is
excellent source of information on scenic byways and backroads less
traveled. Apps like **Roadtrippers** or websites such as **Scenic Byways**
guide you to routes known for their breathtaking views and exciting
landmarks. When planning:

- **Consider the Distance**: Decide how far you're willing to go
  and whether you'll return the same day or turn your drive into
  a weekend getaway.
- **Check Road Conditions**: For less-traveled paths, ensure the
  road is suitable for your vehicle and open for travel.
- **Prepare Your Vehicle**: A quick check-up—tire pressure, oil
  level, and gas tank—can prevent unexpected hitches.

Remember, the drive itself is part of the experience. Allow time for
detours and stops. Sometimes, the most memorable sights are the ones
you stumble upon unexpectedly.

## SAVORING THE MOMENTS

The essence of a scenic drive is to relish the journey. It's tempting to rush from point A to point B, but the heart of the adventure lies in the moments between. Make a point to:

- **Stop for Photos**: Bring a camera or use your smartphone to capture the landscape. These snapshots become the pages of your travel journal, each telling a story.
- **Enjoy a Picnic**: Pack a meal and find a picturesque spot to dine al fresco. A meal with a view is a simple pleasure that elevates the experience.
- **Just Sit and Be**: Find a safe place to pull over and take in the view. Watch the clouds, listen to the sounds of nature, and breathe in the fresh air.

## COMFORT ON THE ROAD

Ensuring your drive is as comfortable as it is scenic makes all the difference. If your vehicle isn't up to the task or you require specific adaptations, renting a car might be the way to go. Many rental agencies offer vehicles with features that cater to various needs—more comfortable seating, better suspension for rougher roads, or advanced navigation systems to keep you on track.

For those who find long drives challenging, consider these adjustments:

- **Ergonomic Accessories**: Seat cushions and back supports can make hours in the car more comfortable.
- **Regular Breaks**: Schedule stops to stretch and move around, keeping the blood flowing and preventing stiffness.
- **Accessible Routes**: If mobility is a concern, focus on drives with plenty of sights from the car or have accessible lookout points.

## BLENDING PASSIONS WITH THE PATH

A scenic drive becomes even more rewarding when intertwined with hobbies or interests. Here are a few ideas to inspire your next road trip:

- **Bird Watching on the Go**: Those binoculars are for more than stationary birding. Many scenic routes pass through habitats teeming with birdlife. Research areas where you might find specific species, turning your drive into a mobile birding adventure.
- **The Photographer's Quest**: Every photographer, amateur or seasoned, knows that light is everything. Plan your drive around the golden hours—early morning or late afternoon—when the light is perfect for capturing the landscape's magic.
- **History in the Hills**: Combine your love for history with scenic drives by mapping out routes that pass through historical sites. Many scenic byways have historical significance, offering glimpses into the past as you meander through the present.

The world outside our windows is a gallery of nature's finest works, from towering mountains and serene lakes to rolling meadows and dense forests. A scenic drive invites you to step into this moving painting to watch each landscape unfold like a live performance where the road is your front-row seat. It's a reminder that beauty isn't just found in distant lands or exotic locations; it's all around us, waiting to be discovered, one mile at a time.

## 4.5  PHOTOGRAPHY WALKS: CAPTURING NATURE

### THROUGH THE LENS

Imagine transforming a simple stroll into an expedition where every step brings a new scene into focus, where the mundane becomes magical through the lens of a camera. Photography walks merge the physical bene-fits of walking with the creative satisfaction of photography. It's not just about snapping pictures; it's about seeing the world anew, finding extraordinary beauty in ordinary places, and telling stories without words.

### CHOOSING YOUR EQUIPMENT

Selecting the right gear is less about having the latest technology and more about understanding what complements your vision and comfort. For some, a smartphone camera offers convenience and surprisingly high-quality images. Modern smartphones have features that rival traditional cameras, including high resolution and various shooting modes. For others, a DSLR or mirrorless camera opens up a world of creative possibilities, with adjustable settings for shutter speed, aperture, and ISO, allowing for more control over the final image.

Consider your goals and the type of photography you're drawn to. Landscape photographers might prioritize wide-angle lenses, while those interested in the more minor details of nature could lean toward macro lenses. Most importantly, choose equipment that feels right for you, something you'll enjoy carrying and using throughout your walk.

## COMPOSING YOUR SHOTS

The essence of a good photograph lies in its composition—the way elements are arranged within the frame. Here are a few tips to elevate your shots:

- **Rule of Thirds**: Envision your image into nine equal parts by two vertical and two horizontal lines. Placing your subject along these lines or at their intersections creates a more balanced and engaging photo.
- **Leading Lines**: Use natural or architectural lines to draw the viewer's eye toward your main subject. Paths, streams, and fences can serve as practical guides.
- **Play with Perspective**: Change your viewpoint to add interest. Crouch down for a ground-level view of a flower or climb higher to capture the sweeping expanse of a landscape.

Lighting also plays a crucial role, with the soft, golden light of early morning and late afternoon offering warmth and depth to your images —experiment with backlighting for silhouettes or side lighting to accentuate textures.

**Ready to add a little zest with some fun?**

---

Q: WHY DID MOTHER NATURE GO TO THERAPY?

A: BECAUSE SHE HAD TOO MANY "CLIMATE" ISSUES TO WORK OUT!

---

# FREE GOODWILL

*"You can't buy happiness, but you can give it, and that's pretty much the same thing."*

UNKNOWN

Hey there,

I have a little favor to ask, and it's all about spreading joy and happiness. You know how good it feels to help someone out, right? That's what I'm hoping you'll do today. I need your help to spread the word!

So, here's the deal: your book review could be the nudge someone needs to start their own adventure. It's like a high-five to a fellow retiree, telling them they've got this!

And the best part? It won't cost you a dime and takes less than a minute. Just scan the QR code or click the link below and share your thoughts

Click Here to Leave a Review!

Imagine the difference your review could make:

- One more retiree is discovering a new hobby that lights up their life.
- One more grandparent finding cool activities to do with their grandkids.
- One more person is transforming their retirement into the adventure of a lifetime.

Thank you from the bottom of my heart. Now, let's get back to having fun!

Your biggest fan,

*Rhonda Gudger*

P.S. - Remember, sharing is caring! If you know another retiree who could use a boost, pass this book along. It's like giving them a virtual high-five!

# CHAPTER 5
# UNLEASHING YOUR INNER CREATOR

---

*"Creativity is the way I share my soul with the world."*

BRENÉ BROWN

---

## 5.1 DISCOVERING YOUR ARTISTIC SIDE

Imagine this: an empty canvas in front of you, filled with endless possibilities, ready to become a mirror of your inner self. The brush dips into the paint, a bright color from an array of choices. Every brushstroke transfers a piece of your soul onto the canvas, narrating stories silently, conveying feelings without a voice. This is the magic of painting and drawing—an art that's as freeing as it is reflective, providing a special mix of self-expression and awareness. Whether you're creating solo or with a fellow artist, I hope it ignites your creative spark.

Think of your creativity as a muscle. Just like any other muscle in your body, it needs exercise to grow stronger. Painting and drawing are perfect for this. They're not about perfection or producing museum-worthy pieces on your first try. It's about letting your imagination run wild, making marks that are uniquely yours, and finding joy in the process. What are the therapeutic benefits? Immense. Picture yourself lost in the rhythm of brushstrokes, the world's noise fading away, leaving a sense of calm and fulfillment in its wake.

## CHOOSING YOUR MEDIUM

Starting your artistic adventure begins with picking your tools. Each medium has its charm and challenges:

- **Watercolors**: Known for their luminous, flowing qualities, they're perfect for capturing landscapes, still life's, or abstract compositions. Remember, watercolors have a mind of their own, often leading to happy accidents that can add unexpected beauty to your work.
- **Acrylics**: These are versatile and forgiving, drying quickly and allowing for layers upon layers. Ideal for experimenting with textures and bold colors.
- **Pencils**: From graphite to colored pencils, they offer precision and control, suitable for detailed work and those who like to sketch on the go.

Your choice might depend on your available space, your budget, and what feels right in your hands. Art stores often have starter kits, allowing you to test the waters without a hefty investment.

## ONLINE TUTORIALS AND CLASSES

The digital age has opened up endless possibilities for learning. Countless artists and instructors share their knowledge online, offering tutorials and classes that cater to every skill level. Websites like

*Skillshare* and *YouTube* are gold mines, packed with lessons on everything from basic drawing techniques to advanced painting tutorials. Here's how to make the most of these resources:

- Schedule regular "art dates" with yourself. Consistency is critical to improvement.
- Start with beginner tutorials, gradually increasing difficulty as your confidence grows.
- Join online art communities. Sharing your progress and receiving feedback can be incredibly motivating.

## CREATING YOUR FIRST MASTERPIECE

Now, for the exciting part—bringing your vision to life. Here's a simple project to get you started, focusing on the joy of creation over perfection:

1. **Choose Your Subject**: Start with something that inspires you, whether it's a landscape, a favorite object, or even your pet.
2. **Sketch Your Outline**: Using a pencil, lightly draw the basic shapes of your subject. This stage is about placement and proportion, not detail.
3. **Select Your Colors**: Think about the mood you want to convey. Warm colors for a vibrant scene? Cool tones for a calm atmosphere?
4. **Paint or Color**: Begin filling in your sketch with broad areas of color, gradually adding layers and details. Remember, it's not about matching reality but expressing how the subject makes you feel.

This project isn't just about finishing a piece of art; it's about experiencing the process, learning from each stroke, and, most importantly, enjoying yourself. So, when you stand back to view your creation, do so with a sense of pride and accomplishment. You've translated thoughts and emotions into something visual and tangible—an act of bravery and self-expression.

Painting and drawing open doors to worlds only you can create, offering a sanctuary for your thoughts and a playground for your imagination. So grab your brush or pencil, and let's turn those blank pages into canvases of expression and windows into our souls.

## 5.2  WRITING: PENNING YOUR LIFE STORIES AND FICTIONAL TALES

Have you thought about writing your autobiography? That book of poetry? Children's books? Our writing bridges the realms of memory and imagination, uniquely capturing the essence of personal experiences while sparking the flames of creativity. It's a process that transforms the intangible—a thought, a feeling, a fleeting moment—into something tangible that can be held, read, and shared. We document our journey through writing, preserving memories that might otherwise fade, and sharing stories that can move, entertain, or inspire others.

## THE POWER OF STORYTELLING

Every person is a natural-born storyteller. Our conversations are filled with anecdotes, our thoughts often wander through imagined scenarios, and our dreams are vibrant narratives. Writing taps into this innate ability, encouraging us to explore the depth of our experiences and the breadth of our imagination. Whether recounting a significant event in your life, creating a fictional world, or expressing your thoughts and feelings, writing is a powerful tool for exploration and expression. It allows us to examine our lives, understand our choices, and connect profoundly with others.

## GETTING STARTED WITH WRITING

Facing a blank page can be daunting, but there are strategies to ease into the writing process and overcome the dreaded writer's block:

- **Keep a Journal**: Jot down daily reflections, exciting thoughts, or memorable events. This habit not only hones your writing skills but also serves as a rich source of material for more structured work.
- **Blogging**: Sharing your insights, stories, or hobbies through a blog allows you to practice writing in a less formal setting. Blogs can be personal or themed, offering a platform to explore subjects you're passionate about.
- **Crafting Short Stories**: Begin with short, manageable pieces. Short stories provide a canvas to experiment with narrative styles, character development, and plot without the commitment of a novel.
- Apps like *Medium* and *Substack* are good platforms to read and write on many topics.

Writing is an iterative process. Your first draft is just that—a first step. Allow yourself the freedom to write poorly, to make mistakes, and to explore. Remember, every writer refines their voice and hone their skills over time.

## WORKSHOPS AND WRITING GROUPS

One of the most rewarding aspects of writing is the opportunity to share your work and receive feedback. Writing workshops and groups offer a supportive environment where writers can learn from each other, gaining new perspectives and insights into their work. These communities can be found in-person and online, catering to various genres and experience levels:

- **Local Workshops**: Many community centers, libraries, and bookstores host writing workshops. These sessions often focus on specific aspects of writing, such as character development, pacing, or dialogue.
- **Online Writing Groups**: Platforms like *Meetup* or *Dedicated Writing Forums* provide spaces for writers to connect, share their work, and participate in critique sessions. Online groups offer the flexibility to engage at your own pace and the advantage of connecting with diverse writers.

Participating in these groups encourages discipline, motivates, and significantly accelerates writing development. The constructive criticism received can be invaluable, helping you to see your work through fresh eyes and identify areas for improvement.

## PUBLISHING YOUR WORK

For many writers, sharing their stories with a broader audience is a dream. With today's technology, publishing your work has never been more accessible. Whether you aim to share your life stories through a memoir, captivate readers with your fiction, or inspire through essays, several paths can lead to publication:

- **Blogs**: An immediate way to reach readers. Platforms like *WordPress* or *Blogger* offer user-friendly options for setting up and customizing your blog, providing a space to publish your work and interact with readers.
- **Self-Publishing Platforms**: Websites like *Amazon's Kindle Direct Publishing (KDP)* or *Smashwords* enable writers to publish e-books and print-on-demand paperbacks. These platforms offer writers control over their work, from setting prices to designing covers.
- **Traditional Publishing**: While more challenging, securing a literary agent and submitting your manuscript to publishing houses can lead to conventional publication. This route often

requires patience and perseverance but can offer broader distribution and professional marketing.

Each publishing path has its benefits and challenges. Consider your goals, resources, and the audience you wish to reach when deciding how to share your work. Remember, sharing your writing is a brave step, opening your inner world to others and inviting them to explore it.

Writing is not just an act of creation; it's an act of sharing. We write to remember, dream, understand, and connect. Whether through journal pages, blog posts, or book chapters, each word we write is a testament to our experiences, imagination, and desire to communicate with the world. As we continue this journey, let's embrace the power of storytelling, the joy of writing, and the courage to share our tales.

## 5.3  DIY PROJECTS: CRAFTING UNIQUE HOME DECOR

Jumping into DIY projects transforms your space and infuses your daily environment with a personal flair. Imagine turning a discarded window frame into a chic picture holder or giving an old chair a new lease on life with just a coat of paint and some creativity. This section guides you to turning ordinary items into extraordinary treasures, making your heart and home a little brighter.

## TAKING THE LEAP INTO DIY

The crux of DIY is seeing potential where others see waste. It's about viewing a room and imagining how you can imprint your essence onto every corner. If the idea of wielding a hammer or a paintbrush seems daunting, fear not. The beauty of DIY lies in its inclusivity; projects exist for every skill level, from novice crafters to seasoned builders. The key is starting small. Your confidence will grow with every successful project, encouraging you to tackle more ambitious endeavors.

## PROJECT INSPIRATIONS FOR EVERY CRAFTER

Here's a spectrum of ideas to spark your creativity, regardless of your experience:

### FOR BEGINNERS:

- Mason jar herb gardens bring greenery and flavor to your kitchen sill.
- Personalized coasters crafted from ceramic tiles, using decoupage or permanent markers, add a personal touch to your coffee table.

### INTERMEDIATE PROJECTS:

- A ladder shelf made from reclaimed wood offers a rustic space for books and knick-knacks.
- Transforming an old suitcase into a quirky side table injects vintage charm into any room.

### ADVANCED ENDEAVORS:

- Building a window seat creates a cozy nook for reading and relaxation.
- Crafting a mosaic backsplash from broken tiles gives your kitchen a vibrant facelift.

## GATHERING YOUR TOOLKIT

Before diving into your project, assembling your toolkit is crucial. Basic supplies often include:

- Safety gear such as gloves and goggles
- A reliable set of screwdrivers
- A hammer, nails, and screws
- Sandpaper for smoothing rough edges
- Paint and brushes for a splash of color
- A hot glue gun for quick adhesion

Refrain from having everything from the get-go. Part of the DIY journey is learning what tools work best for you. Local hardware stores and online tutorials can offer advice on what's essential for your chosen project. Additionally, consider borrowing tools from friends or neighbors to save costs and foster community connections.

## SHOWCASING YOUR HANDIWORK

Once your project is complete, sharing it can be as rewarding as the crafting process itself. Here are ways to celebrate and display your achievements:

- **Social Media**: Platforms like Instagram and Pinterest are ideal for showcasing your projects. Use hashtags to join broader DIY conversations and gain inspiration from fellow enthusiasts.
- **Craft Fairs**: Local craft fairs offer a platform to display your work, connect with other crafters, and sell some creations.
- **Gift Giving**: Handcrafted items make heartfelt gifts imbued with your invested time and love. Whether it's a hand-painted vase or a bespoke piece of furniture, gifting your DIY projects brings joy to you and the recipient.

- Etsy: If you're truly dedicated and want to do some business, you could always open an Etsy store and sell your wares!

The essence of DIY isn't just about the final product; it's about the process, the learning curve, and the satisfaction of breathing new life into forgotten items. It's a celebration of creativity, resourcefulness, and personal expression that resonates through every brush stroke, every nail driven, and every piece of fabric sewn. So, grab your tools, gather your materials, and let the transformation begin.

## 5.4 COOKING CLASSES: EXPLORING NEW CUISINES FROM HOME

The kitchen, often called the heart of the home, becomes a place of endless discovery and delight when we introduce new recipes and techniques into our cooking routines. A special kind of joy bubbles up when you nail a dish from a cuisine you've never tried. It's akin to a culinary adventure without needing a passport or luggage.

## THE SATISFACTION OF CULINARY EXPLORATION

Exploring and preparing international cuisines can expand both your taste buds and your worldview. Each recipe tells a story, each ingredient a character, and each technique a plot twist. The act of cooking, therefore, transforms into an engaging narrative where you're both the author and the audience. Think of the satisfaction from successfully intertwining flavors you once thought were beyond your culinary grasp. It's about big and small triumphs, from folding dumplings perfectly to achieving the right simmer on a stew that's been simmering for hours.

## WHERE TO FIND ONLINE COOKING CLASSES

Our digital era has made learning from chefs and home cooks worldwide incredibly easy. Websites like *MasterClass* feature lessons from renowned chefs, offering insights into recipes and their philosophies. Meanwhile, platforms like *Udemy* and *Coursera* provide various cooking courses, covering everything from baking basics to advanced culinary techniques. For a more interactive experience, consider live classes on Zoom or Instagram, where you can cook alongside the instructor and ask questions in real-time:

- **MasterClass** highlights include Gordon Ramsay teaching restaurant-inspired dishes and Massimo Bottura exploring modern Italian cooking.
- **Udemy** offers courses like "Essential Cooking Skills" and "Artisan Bread Making," catering to varied interests.
- **Coursera** partners with universities and culinary schools to bring structured courses focusing on nutrition and culinary science.

## STARTING SIMPLE

Starting this culinary adventure doesn't mean you have to dive head-first into the most complex dishes. On the contrary, beginning with straightforward recipes can build your confidence. Look for dishes with fewer ingredients and steps or those that use your already familiar cooking equipment. Gradually introduce more complex techniques or unfamiliar ingredients as you grow more comfortable. This gradual progression turns the learning process into an enjoyable journey rather than a daunting task.

- **Simple Starters**: Dishes like pasta aglio e olio or a classic stir-fry offer a foundation to build upon, focusing on mastering basic cooking techniques.
- **Progression**: As confidence grows, explore recipes introducing new techniques or ingredients, such as homemade sushi rolls or a basic curry.

## COOKING TOGETHER, APART

In times when gathering around a table with friends or family might not be possible, virtual cook-alongs present a fantastic alternative. These sessions make cooking a shared experience and an opportunity for connection and laughter. Setting up is straightforward—choose a recipe, send out invites, and meet online at the designated time. As everyone follows the same recipe, you'll find yourselves navigating the cooking process together, sharing tips and, inevitably, some amusing mishaps:

- **Theme Nights**: Add more fun by theming your cook-along, "Taco Tuesday" or "Mediterranean Meanderings."
- **Show and Tell**: Present your dishes to each other at the end of the session. It's a great way to celebrate your efforts and discuss what you've learned.

Every diced vegetable, seared piece of meat, or perfectly baked loaf of bread lies a story of tradition, culture, and personal growth. Cooking classes, especially those that introduce us to new cuisines, invite us into these stories, offering a taste of the world from the comfort of our kitchens. They remind us that cooking is more than a daily necessity; it's a canvas for creativity exploration and a way to unite people, even when they're miles apart.

## 5.5  GENEALOGY: UNCOVERING YOUR FAMILY HISTORY

Exploring your family history is like opening a book filled with stories waiting to be uncovered. There's a profound sense of connection in learning about the lives of your ancestors, understanding your origins, and seeing yourself as part of an ongoing story that spans generations. This journey into genealogy is more than just collecting names and dates; it's about linking with your past and discovering the intricate web of experiences that have led to your existence today.

## TALKING TO RELATIVES

When you decide to explore your roots, the first step might seem simple but is incredibly rich in potential: talking to relatives. Family gatherings can be transformed into informal interview sessions, where stories about the older generations come to life. Every photograph, letter, and heirloom has a story, often untold, waiting for someone willing to listen. This process enriches your understanding of your family's past and strengthens bonds with living relatives, creating a shared sense of heritage and identity.

## INTERNET RESEARCH

The internet has revolutionized genealogical research, making it easier than ever to trace your family tree. A wealth of resources, databases, and tools are now at your fingertips, many of which are free or offer trial periods. Websites like *Ancestry.com* and *FamilySearch.org* serve as gateways to millions of historical records, from census data to military registrations. Meanwhile, platforms like *MyHeritage* offer DNA testing services, providing insights into your ethnic origins and connecting you with distant relatives. Here are a few tips for navigating these resources:

- Start with what you know, gradually working your way back. Begin with your immediate family and use official documents to confirm details.
- Use multiple sources to cross-verify information. Records can sometimes contain errors, so it's wise to look for confirmation from different documents.
- Keep an open mind. Families are complex, and history is often surprising. Be prepared for unexpected discoveries along the way.

As your research unfolds, documenting and preserving your findings becomes crucial. Creating a digital family tree can be a practical way to organize information, with software like *Gramps* or *Legacy Family Tree* offering robust tools for recording details, storing documents, and generating reports. Consider compiling a family history book with stories, photographs, and copies of original documents for a more tangible connection to the past. This can be a cherished heirloom, a definite link between past, present, and future generations.

## SHARING YOUR FAMILY TREE

Genealogical discoveries can be incredibly rewarding, offering family members a sense of belonging and understanding of their heritage. Here are a few ways to share your findings:

- Host a family history night, where you present your research, share stories, and discuss findings.
- Create a private family website or social media group dedicated to your genealogical journey, encouraging relatives to contribute stories and information.
- Donate copies of your research to family archives or local history societies, ensuring the preservation and accessibility of your family's story for future generations.

In the end, tracing your genealogy is more than just a hobby; it's a deeply personal quest that can reveal as much about yourself as it does about your ancestors. It's a way to honor those who came before you, preserving their memories and stories for those who will follow. As you uncover the stories of your family's past, you might find that the journey itself is as rewarding as the destination, filled with moments of discovery, connection, and reflection.

**It's time for a pinch of playfulness:**

---

Q: WHY DID THE INNER CREATOR BRING A PENCIL TO BED?

A: BECAUSE THEY WANTED TO SKETCH THEIR DREAMS!

# CHAPTER 6
# LIFELONG LEARNING UNLOCKED

*"The beautiful thing about learning is that nobody can take it away from you."*

**B.B. KING**

Remember the thrill of peeling open the first page of a new notebook? That crisp, fresh promise of beginning something new? For many, it's a sensation that gets lost in the shuffle of daily responsibilities. Yet, the allure of learning—discovering new concepts, mastering fresh skills, or simply indulging in  the joy of a new hobby—never truly fades. It waits patiently for us to turn back its way, offering a richness to life that's both invigorating and deeply fulfilling.

Let's dust off that sense of anticipation and excitement. Learning isn't confined to the four walls of a classroom or the years before retirement. It's a lifelong endeavor that's incredibly enriching and accessible in retirement. Whether diving into a subject you've always been curious about or finally having the time to devote to a passion project, expanding your knowledge can be thrilling and immensely rewarding.

## 6.1 LOCAL COMMUNITY COLLEGE COURSES: LEARNING IN A SOCIAL ENVIRONMENT

### THE VALUE OF IN-PERSON LEARNING

There's something irreplaceable about learning in a group setting. The energy of a shared space, the immediate feedback from instructors and peers, and the spontaneous discussions that spring up offer a dynamic learning experience that's hard to replicate. It's not just about the information absorbed; it's about the connections formed, the perspectives gained, and the community built. Plus, there's the added benefit of structure—having a set time and place for classes helps create a routine, making it easier to commit and stick with.

### EXPLORING COURSE OFFERINGS

Your local community college is a treasure trove of learning opportunities, often with diverse courses designed with retirees in mind. These institutions cater to various interests, from the arts and history to technology and gardening. Here's how to tap into this resource:

- **Visit the College Website**: Most colleges have a section for community education or courses for older adults. This is a great starting point to explore what's available.
- **Talk to an Advisor**: If you need help figuring out where to begin, a chat with an educational advisor can help guide you toward courses that align with your interests and goals.

- **Attend an Open House**: Many colleges host open houses for community education programs. It's a chance to meet instructors, ask questions, and even sample mini-lessons.

## ACCESSIBILITY AND AFFORDABILITY

Community colleges know education is not a one-size-fits-all endeavor, especially for retirees. Many institutions offer courses at reduced rates for older adults or even free classes designed to be accessible and enjoyable without the pressure of exams or grades. Scholarships or financial aid options may also be available to help cover costs, making learning more accessible to everyone.

## MAXIMIZING THE EXPERIENCE

Enrolling in a course is just the beginning. Here's how to make the most of this opportunity:

- **Engage Fully**: Take your time in class discussions or group projects. Your life experiences offer valuable insights that can enrich everyone's learning environment.
- **Join a Club or Group**: Many colleges have clubs or groups related to course subjects. These can be fantastic ways to dive deeper into a topic, meet like-minded individuals, and apply what you're learning in a practical setting.
- **Be Open to New Experiences**: Allow yourself to be a beginner again. It's okay to know only some things from the start. Embrace the learning process with an open heart and mind.

This chapter isn't just about encouraging you to learn; it's about unlocking the doors to a world brimming with possibilities and opportunities for growth, connection, and fulfillment. Whether through a painting class that unveils a hidden talent or a history course that sparks a newfound passion, the journey of learning is boundless, enriching our minds and lives. So, let's step into this adventure with curiosity and enthusiasm, ready to discover all the wonders that await.

## 6.2 ONLINE COURSES: EDUCATION AT YOUR FINGERTIPS

The digital age has opened doors to a world where learning is not bound by geography or time zones. The internet is a wash with plat-

forms offering courses on everything from astrophysics to zen gardening, all available from the comfort of your living room. It's a buffet of knowledge, with the freedom to sample a little bit of everything or deep-dive into a subject that tugs at your curiosity.

## ONLINE LEARNING PLATFORMS

When exploring the vast array of online learning platforms, choosing the one that best suits your needs can be like picking the ideal book from a library. Each platform has its flavor, specialties, and ways of delivering content. For instance, **Coursera** partners with universities to offer free and paid courses that often include certification. Meanwhile, platforms like **Udemy** focus on a vast range of topics taught by industry professionals, providing lifetime access to courses you've enrolled in. Then there's Khan Academy, a free resource that excels in foundational subjects, perfect for brushing up on basics or exploring new areas of interest.

### Schedule Your Learning

When pinpointing a course that sparks your interest, the next step is weaving it into your daily or weekly routine. Setting aside dedicated time for learning ensures you make consistent progress. Think of it as setting an appointment with your future self, where the agenda is expansion and growth. Here are a few strategies to keep you on track:

- **Calendar Blocks**: Just **as** you might schedule a doctor's appointment or coffee with a friend, block off time in your calendar for your course.
- **Routine Integration**: Tie your learning sessions to a part of your existing routine, for example, after your morning walk or right before lunch.
- **Goal Setting**: Break your course into manageable goals. Completing a module, finishing a chapter, or even spending a set amount of time studying can all be milestones.

## SHARING WHAT YOU'VE LEARNED

Now, imagine you've acquired this new knowledge or skill. What comes next? Applying what you've learned cements your understanding and allows you to share the fruits of your effort with the world. If you've taken a course in digital photography, consider setting up a small exhibit at a local community center or online. Have you dipped your toes into the basics of web development? Maybe it's time to build that personal website or blog you've been thinking about. Even more fulfilling can be using your new skills to give back—tutoring students in your newfound subject or offering your expertise to local non-profits.

The beauty of online courses lies not just in the learning but in the ripple effects that knowledge can create. It's about the doors you open, not just in your mind but the world around you, transforming learning from a solitary pursuit into a shared journey.

## 6.3  BOOK CLUBS: EXPANDING HORIZONS THROUGH READING

Getting lost in a great book can take you to different realms, plunge you into exciting escapades, or acquaint you with unforgettable characters. However, the joy of reading multiplies when shared with others. That's where book clubs come into play, turning the solitary act of reading into a collective exploration of literature. In these gatherings, stories serve as springboards for deeper discussions, challenging perspectives, and fostering connections among members.

## THE BENEFITS OF BOOK CLUBS

Participating in a book club enriches your reading experience in several ways. Firstly, it broadens your literary horizons, nudging you to pick up books you might not have considered otherwise. This exposure can be delightfully surprising, leading you to discover new favorite genres or authors. Moreover, discussing a book with others can deepen your understanding and appreciation. Hearing different interpretations of a character's motives or a plot twist can offer new insights and enhance your enjoyment of the story. Lastly, book clubs are fantastic for building social connections. They bring together people with a shared interest in reading, providing a regular opportunity to meet new friends and engage in stimulating conversation.

## STARTING OR JOINING A BOOK CLUB

If you want to join a book club, you might wonder where to find one or how to get started. Here are some steps to guide you:

- **Check Local Libraries and Bookstores**: Many libraries and bookstores host book clubs that welcome new members. These can be great options as they often provide a structured setting and sometimes even offer books for upcoming discussions.
- **Look Online**: Websites like *Meetup.com* can help find local book clubs. You might also find clubs that align with specific interests, such as mystery novels, historical fiction, or biographies.
- **Start Your Own**: If you can't find a club that suits your needs, consider starting one. Reach out to friends who enjoy reading or advertise in local community centers. Decide on the

logistics, like how often you'll meet and where, and you're good to go.

Choosing books and facilitating discussion might seem daunting if you start your club. Here are a few tips to make the process smoother:

- **Choose Books Collectively**: Allow members to suggest and vote on books. This ensures everyone has a say and increases the likelihood of members engaging with the choice.
- **Prepare Discussion Questions**: To facilitate conversation, having a list of discussion questions or topics is helpful. Many books come with discussion guides, and additional resources can be found online.

## VIRTUAL BOOK CLUBS

The rise of virtual book clubs has made it easier than ever to connect with fellow readers, no matter where they are. These clubs use video chat services to discuss books, allowing flexibility and convenience. Members can join from the comfort of their homes, making it more straightforward to fit meetings into busy schedules.

- **Selecting a Platform**: Common choices include *Zoom*, *Skype*, or *Google Meet*. Choose a platform that's accessible and easy for all members to use.
- **Managing Discussions**: Virtual settings can make it challenging for everyone to speak up. Assigning a moderator for each meeting can help manage the flow of conversation and ensure everyone has a chance to contribute.

## DIVERSE READING SELECTIONS

One of the highlights of participating in book clubs is the chance to explore a diverse range of literature. Promoting a variety of book selections can enhance conversations and provide a more expansive perspective on the world.

Consider rotating genres, picking books from different countries or cultures, or alternating between fiction and non-fiction. This variety keeps the meetings exciting and promotes a deeper understanding and empathy for different perspectives and life experiences.

- **Themed Months**: To introduce diversity, some clubs dedicate certain months to specific themes, such as "Women Authors Month" or "Global Literature Month."
- **Guest Speakers**: Occasionally, invite authors, experts, or enthusiasts to discuss the book or related topics. This can add a unique dimension to your discussions and provide valuable insights.

In essence, book clubs are vibrant communities where stories are shared and dissected, offering members a chance to venture beyond their reading comfort zones, challenge their thinking, and form meaningful connections. Whether in person or online, these clubs celebrate the power of literature to bring people together, sparking conversations that linger long after the last page is turned.

## 6.4  LANGUAGE LEARNING: EMBRACING NEW CULTURES

Starting the adventure of mastering a new language opens up more than just the ability to order coffee in Paris or ask for directions in Tokyo. It's like receiving a key to unlock doors worldwide, not just to places but to people, cultures, and experiences. The adventure of learning a new language is both a mental exercise and a heart-opening journey, allowing us to connect with others on a more profound level.

## THE JOY OF LANGUAGE LEARNING

Imagine the thrill of finally **understanding** a song in Spanish or watching a Japanese film without subtitles. Beyond these joys, language learning offers significant cognitive and cultural benefits. It sharpens the mind, enhances multitasking skills, and even delays cognitive aging. Perhaps more importantly, it fosters empathy and understanding. As we learn a new language, we also gain insights into the culture and worldview of its speakers, breaking down barriers and building bridges in their stead.

## CHOOSING A LANGUAGE TO LEARN

Choosing which language to learn can feel like standing at a cross-roads, with countless paths sprawling out in front of you. Consider these signposts to guide your choice:

- **Personal Interest**: Is there a culture you've always been fascinated by? Let your passions lead the way.
- **Cultural Heritage**: Learning the language of your ancestors can be a gratifying way to connect with your roots.
- **Practicality**: Considerations like travel plans or career opportunities can sometimes steer your decision.
- **Learning Resources**: Some languages have more learning materials available. Consider the ease of accessing resources and communities to support your learning.

## TOOLS AND RESOURCES FOR LANGUAGE LEARNERS

Thankfully, the digital age has made language learning more accessible than ever. Here's a roundup of tools to kickstart your linguistic adventure:

- **Language Learning Apps**: *Duolingo*, *Babbel,* and *Rosetta Stone* offer interactive lessons that make learning fun and manageable, even for busy schedules.
- **Online Courses**: Platforms like *Coursera* and *edX* provide more structured courses, often designed by universities and language experts.
- **Language Exchange Communities**: Websites like *Tandem* and *HelloTalk* connect you with native speakers around the globe, allowing for mutual language practice.

Incorporating language learning into your daily routine can be simple. Listen to a podcast in your target language while cooking dinner, swap your evening TV show for a series in that language, or start your day with a quick lesson on your favorite language app. Small, consistent efforts can lead to significant progress over time.

## PRACTICING WITH NATIVE SPEAKERS

Interacting with native speakers is a game-changer in language learning. It's where the rubber meets the road, testing what you've learned in the real world. Here are some ways to dive into practice:

- **Language Exchange Meetups**: Many cities have language exchange groups where learners meet to practice speaking. It's a great way to meet new people and immerse yourself in conversation.
- **Online Conversation Partners**: If local groups aren't an option, online platforms can pair you with conversation partners for virtual practice sessions.
- **Travel**: Immersing yourself in a place where your target language is spoken is the most exhilarating way to learn. Even short trips can boost your confidence and fluency.
- **Volunteer Work**: Look for opportunities to volunteer with communities that speak the language you're learning. This

gives you practice and enriches your understanding of the culture.

Each new word learned, every sentence constructed, and the countless mistakes made along the way, are all steps toward linguistic proficiency and a broader, more inclusive view of the world.

## 6.5  DISCOVERING THE JOY OF MUSIC

Music, with its universal appeal, becomes an integral part of our lives, reflecting our emotions and telling our stories without words. Learning to play a musical instrument offers a unique way to tap into this expressive power, enriching both the soul and the mind. It's a path filled with discovery, challenges, and the joy of creating something beautiful.

## EMBRACE THE SYMPHONY OF LEARNING

Playing an instrument is a dance between discipline and freedom; it requires practice and patience but rewards with unbridled joy and emotional release. Studies have shown that music education can enhance cognitive functions, improve memory, and boost mood. It's a workout for the brain as much as for the heart, making it an ideal pursuit for anyone looking to keep both sharp and open.

## SELECTING YOUR MUSICAL COMPANION

Choosing an instrument is the first step on this melodious path and should reflect your musical tastes, lifestyle, and physical considerations. Here are a few pointers to guide your choice:

- **Interest and Genre**: Let your musical preferences guide you. The violin or piano might be your call if classical music stirs your soul. Jazz enthusiasts might gravitate towards the saxophone or trumpet.
- **Physical Comfort**: Consider the physical demands of the instrument. Those with joint issues find keyboard instruments more comfortable, while others prefer the tactile nature of string instruments like the guitar or ukulele.
- **Space and Environment**: The size of the instrument and the sound level should fit your living situation. Electronic instruments like keyboards can be played with headphones, making them apartment-friendly.

## NAVIGATING THE SEA OF LESSONS AND SUPPORT

With your instrument chosen, the next step is finding guidance and instruction to start your musical journey. The abundance of resources available today makes learning more accessible than ever:

- **Local Music Teachers**: Personalized instruction can accelerate your learning. Look for teachers through local music schools or community centers.
- **Online Tutorials and Courses**: Sites like *YouTube* host countless tutorials for free, while platforms like MasterClass feature lessons by renowned musicians.
- **Music Groups and Community Bands**: Joining a local music group or community band can provide a supportive environment to practice and learn from fellow music enthusiasts.

## THE SWEET REWARDS OF MUSICAL PRACTICE

The road to musical proficiency is paved with patience and persever-ance, but the milestones bring immense satisfaction. From mastering your first song to sharing your music with others, each achievement fuels your passion and encourages further exploration. Here are some of the rewards that await:

- **Personal Fulfillment**: There's a deep sense of achievement in seeing your skills progress in expressing yourself through music.
- **Social Connections**: Music has a way of bringing people together. Joining bands or ensembles enhances your skills and builds lasting friendships.
- **Emotional Expression**: Playing an instrument offers an outlet for emotions, a way to channel feelings into something tangible and resonant.
- **Cultural Exploration**: Learning music from different parts of the world can broaden your cultural understanding and appreciation.

Ultimately, learning to play a musical instrument opens up a world of emotional and cognitive benefits. It's a pursuit that enriches your life, offering a unique blend of challenge and joy, discipline, and freedom. As you progress, the notes you play become more than just sounds; they reflect your journey, expressions of your inner world, and connections to the vast tapestry of human experience.

**Now let's have a little fun:**

Q: WHY DON'T LIFELONG LEARNERS EVER GET LOST?

A: BECAUSE THEY ALWAYS FIND THEMSELVES IN A NEW BOOK!

# CHAPTER 7

# SHARING YOUR SPARK: VOLUNTEER WORK AND COMMUNITY ENGAGEMENT

---

*"The best way to find yourself is to lose yourself in the service of others."*

**MAHATMA GANDHI**

---

Imagine your hands not just as tools for daily tasks but as instruments of change, capable of painting smiles, crafting hope, and building bridges within your community. It's about transforming the ordinary into the extraordinary, one act of kindness at a time. This is the essence of volunteer work—a medium through which the fabric of society  becomes more prosperous, more colorful, and infinitely more connected.

## 7.1 FINDING FULFILLMENT IN HELPING OTHERS

Volunteering is like planting seeds in a garden you rarely visit, yet every time you do, you're greeted by a lush landscape of growth, color, and life. It's about contributing to something larger than oneself and witnessing the ripple effects of your actions. From reading books to children at the local library to serving meals at a homeless shelter, every act of volunteering is a thread in the larger tapestry of community well-being.

- **Local Libraries**: Often in need of volunteers for reading programs, organizations, and events. It is a perfect spot if you love books and believe in literacy as a cornerstone of education.
- **Food Banks and Shelters**: These institutions are always looking for individuals willing to lend a hand, whether sorting donations or preparing meals.
- **Environmental Clean-Ups**: Join local groups in efforts to beautify parks, beaches, or community spaces. It's a tangible way to see the impact of your efforts.

## THE SOCIAL ASPECT OF VOLUNTEERING

The beauty of volunteering lies in the work done and the connections formed. Picture a scenario where you meet someone with a different background or life story during a community clean-up. This interaction broadens your perspective and could lead to lasting friendships based on shared values and experiences. These social bonds often become the unsung rewards of volunteer work, enriching your life beyond the immediate satisfaction of helping out.

## IMPACT BEYOND WORK

Volunteering does more than fill gaps in community services; it knits the fabric of the community tighter. Take, for instance, a local after-school program where volunteers mentor young students. The direct impact is visible in improved grades and student morale. But look closer; you'll see parents feeling supported, teachers gaining valuable allies, and volunteers discovering new passions or career paths. This domino effect elevates volunteering from mere service to a catalyst for communal growth and personal transformation.

## LEARNING VOLUNTEER OPPORTUNITIES

Finding the right volunteer opportunity is like browsing a menu at a new restaurant; everything looks inviting, but what will satisfy your appetite for making a difference? Here are some tips to guide your choice:

- **Reflect on Your Interests**: Matching your hobbies or passions with volunteer work can make the experience more fulfilling. Love the outdoors? Consider environmental conservation efforts.
- **Assess Your Skills**: Professional background or life skills can be invaluable. Accountants can help non-profits with bookkeeping, while avid gardeners can contribute to community gardens.
- **Use Online Platforms**: Websites like VolunteerMatch.org and Idealist.org act as matchmakers, connecting volunteers with opportunities that align with their interests and skills.
- **Try A Few Organizations Before Committing:** Give yourself time to find the organization and team, then decide where to spend your valuable time.

Volunteering is an avenue for growth, connection, and contribution, painting a picture of a community where every individual holds the brush to improve the collective canvas. It's a testament to the power of shared efforts and the beauty of working together toward common goals. So, roll up your sleeves, step into your community's garden, and see what blooms from your contributions.

## 7.2  JOINING HOBBY CLUBS: SHARING INTERESTS AND SKILLS

Picture this: a place where your interests spark, skills grow, and every high-five weaves into the shared story of a club. It's right around the corner in the world of hobby groups.

Whether it's the delicate dance of knitting needles, the strategic placement of a chess piece, or the spirited discussions of a book club, these groups offer a haven for enthusiasts to come together and revel in their shared interests.

### FINDING SHARED INTERESTS

The allure of **hobby** clubs lies in their ability to bring together individuals who share a common passion. Picture this: a room filled with the vibrant chatter of avid gardeners swapping tips on nurturing orchids or the quiet concentration of model train enthusiasts discussing the nuances of historic locomo-
tives. Here, age is just a number, and the joy of shared interests transcends generations, creating a vibrant community of learners and teachers:

- **Gardening Clubs**: Where green thumbs flourish, sharing knowledge on everything from composting to container gardening.
- **Chess Clubs**: A battleground of minds, where strategies are discussed and friendships are forged over the board.
- **Book Clubs**: Literary havens where stories are dissected and perspectives are broadened with every page turned.

Every member brings a piece of themselves in these spaces, a snippet of their life's tapestry, enriching the club with diverse experiences and insights.

## STARTING YOUR CLUB

Sometimes, the club you dream of doesn't exist nearby. Why not plant the seed yourself? Initiating your hobby club can be a thrilling adventure where you're the captain steering the ship toward uncharted waters. Here's how to embark on this rewarding voyage:

- **Identify Your Niche**: Pinpoint the focus of your club. It could be as broad as "crafting" or as specific as "watercolor landscapes."
- **Spread the Word**: Use local community boards, social media, or word of mouth to attract members. Remember to underestimate the power of a catchy flyer at your local coffee shop.
- **Organize the Logistics**: Decide on the frequency of meetings, a suitable venue, and how the club will be structured. Will each session have a leader, or will members take turns?
- **Set the Agenda**: Initial meetings can be used to gauge members' interests and set goals for the club. It's about creating a roadmap that reflects everyone's aspirations.

Creating a club from scratch is akin to nurturing a garden; it takes patience, care, and a lot of love, but the blossoms are well worth the effort.

## LEARNING AND GROWING TOGETHER

The magic of hobby clubs isn't just in the shared interests but in the collective growth within these groups. It's a space where beginners and veterans can learn from each other, where skills are taught and shared with love and enthusiasm. Picture a novice knitter struggling with their first scarf, being guided by the seasoned hands of a fellow member, or a budding photographer receiving constructive feedback from peers. This environment of mutual support and learning fosters individual growth and strengthens the bonds within the club, creating a family of sorts.

- **Skill-Sharing Sessions**: Regularly dedicate time for members to teach a specific skill or technique.
- **Guest Speakers**: Invite experts or enthusiasts outside the club to share their knowledge and experiences.
- **Challenge Projects**: Set up group projects or challenges, encouraging members to apply their skills and learn new ones.

In these gatherings, every question asked is a step towards mastery, and every piece of advice given is a gift, enriching the club's collective knowledge pool.

**Club Activities and Events**

Keeping the spark alive in a hobby club involves more than just regular meetings; it's about creating moments that members look forward to, events that become the highlights of their social calendar. These activities strengthen the camaraderie within the club and showcase the club's talents and achievements to the broader community:

- **Exhibitions and Showcases**: Organize events where members can display their work, be it a photography exhibit, a craft fair, or a musical performance.
- **Workshops**: Host workshops that allow members to dive deeper into specific aspects of the hobby, maybe even trying their hand at teaching.
- **Field Trips**: Plan outings related to the club's focus, like a visit to a botanical garden for gardening clubs or a historical site for history lovers.
- **Community Projects**: Engage in projects that benefit the

community, such as public art installations, charity auctions, or literacy programs.

Each activity is a thread in the vibrant tapestry of the club's story, adding colors of joy, achievement, and togetherness. It's about creating a legacy of shared passions and collective triumphs, a testament to the power of coming together over shared interests and aspirations.

## 7.3 TRAVEL GROUPS: EXPLORING NEW DESTINATIONS TOGETHER

Picture this: you're standing at the edge of the Grand Canyon, amazed by the sheer magnitude and beauty before you. Now, imagine turning to share that wonder with a group of friends who are just as captivated as you are. This is the heart of group travel: moments of shared awe, laughter that echo through historic streets, and collective gasps as you witness the Northern Lights dance across the sky. These experiences, amplified by the joy of sharing them, make traveling in a group uniquely rewarding.

Traveling together offers a bouquet of benefits that solo journeys might not. For starters, there's comfort in numbers, providing a sense of security as you navigate unfamiliar territories. Then there's the logistical ease; group travel often comes with itineraries that smooth out planning bumps, allowing you to immerse yourself fully in the experience. But the most cherished aspect is the camaraderie, the chance to forge new friendships or deepen existing ones, creating bonds that last long after you've returned home.

## FINDING THE RIGHT TRAVEL GROUP

Selecting a travel group that aligns with your interests and style is critical to ensuring a harmonious journey. For retirees or those inching closer to this chapter of life, groups that cater specifically to your age bracket can offer itineraries that balance adventure with comfort, providing experiences that are both enriching and accessible. Here's how you can find your travel tribe:

- **Specialty Travel Forums and Websites**: Online communities dedicated to travel often have sections for group travel, where you can find postings from organizations or clubs that arrange trips for specific interest groups, including retirees.
- **Local Community Centers or Clubs**: Many community organizations have travel clubs that organize regular trips. These can be great options for those looking to start with shorter, local trips to gauge their comfort level before venturing further.
- **Social Media**: Platforms like Facebook have countless groups where members share travel opportunities. Searching for "travel groups for retirees" or "senior travel clubs" can yield numerous options.

When considering a travel group, take a moment to reach out to the organizers. Ask about past trips, the average age and interests of participants, and details about the itinerary. This can help ensure the group's pace and activities align with your desired goals.

## PLANNING GROUP TRIPS

The logistics of planning a trip with a group, significantly when interests and energy levels may vary, can seem daunting. Yet, this process can also be part of the fun, a collaborative effort that builds anticipation for the journey ahead. Here are some tips to navigate this stage smoothly:

- **Open Dialogue**: Early discussions about everyone's must-see sights and activities help ensure the itinerary has something for everyone. It's about finding the right balance that respects both the adventurous spirits and those seeking relaxation.

- **Budgeting**: Group travel often comes with the perk of shared costs, but it's essential to be upfront about budgets. Tools like shared spreadsheets can help track expenses and ensure transparency.
- **Flexibility**: While having a plan is crucial, so is flexibility. Unexpected events can lead to some of the best memories, from a rainy day to a hidden gem on the beaten path.

Assigning roles based on each person's strengths can also streamline planning. Someone with a knack for research can look into accommodations, while another, perhaps with a linguistic flair, could handle communications in destinations where the local language might pose a barrier.

## CREATING LASTING MEMORIES

The memories made on group trips often become the stories we recount for years, shared experiences that weave into the fabric of our friendships. To capture and honor these moments:

- **Photo Journals**: Encourage everyone to take photos and then compile these into a shared album or a scrapbook. This not only preserves memories but also showcases the journey from multiple perspectives.
- **Group Reflections**: Setting aside time during the trip to share highlights or funny moments can be a meaningful way to acknowledge the shared experience. Whether it's over a meal or a casual gathering, these reflections can deepen the sense of camaraderie.
- **Reunion Gatherings**: Once back home, organizing a get-together to relive the trip can keep the post-travel blues at bay. It's also an opportunity to start dreaming up your next adventure together.

In group travel, every shared sunset, every laughter-filled bus ride, and every awe-inspiring sight becomes a thread in the shared tapestry of your experiences. It's about more than just the places you visit; it's about the people you're with and the bonds that form, making each destination a backdrop to the stories you create together.

**Now a bit of light-hearted fun:**

---

Q: WHY DID THE VOLUNTEER JOIN THE COMMUNITY GARDEN?

A: BECAUSE THEY WANTED TO PLANT SEEDS OF CHANGE AND WATCH THEIR COMMUNITY BLOSSOM!

---

# CHAPTER 8

# CULTIVATING CONNECTIONS IN THE DIGITAL AGE

*"Technology enables us to reach out to others, but it's the human touch that truly unites us."*

**SIMON SINEK**

Imagine your garden. Now, consider each plant a different interest or hobby you've nurtured. Some are robust, thriving with minimal care, while others need more attention to blossom. Much like this garden, the digital landscape is lush with communities and groups that resonate with your diverse  interests, waiting for you to join and flourish together. From the comfort of your home, you can connect with fellow enthusiasts across the globe, sharing insights, laughter, and support. This chapter is all about finding your group online and making the most of these connections.

## 8.1  SOCIAL MEDIA GROUPS: FINDING YOUR GROUP ONLINE

### NAVIGATING SOCIAL MEDIA PLATFORMS

Choosing the right social media platform is like picking the perfect soil for your plants; it's essential for growth. With its vast array of groups, **Facebook** caters to nearly every interest imaginable — from knitting aficionados to space enthusiasts. **Instagram** provides a visual feast, perfect for photography lovers and travel buffs to share and explore. Meanwhile, **LinkedIn** is a professional networking haven that is ideal for industry-specific groups and career advice. Here's how to dig in:

- Start with platforms you're already familiar with to ease the transition.
- Use the search function to find groups by keywords related to your interests.
- Look at the group's description, member count, and post frequency to gauge its activity and relevance to your interests.

### ENGAGING WITH ONLINE COMMUNITIES

It's time to engage once you've found a group that piques your interest. Think of it like watering your plants — regular and thoughtful care leads to the best growth. Here are some ways to engage effectively:

- Introduce yourself upon joining. Share a bit about why you're excited to be part of the group.
- Participate in discussions by commenting on posts that interest you. Share your insights, ask questions, and offer support.
- Remember, quality over quantity. Engaging meaningfully in a few discussions is better than spreading yourself too thin.

## SAFETY AND PRIVACY ONLINE

As you would protect your garden from pests, safeguarding your privacy online is paramount. Here's how:

- Adjust your privacy settings to control who sees your posts and personal information.
- Be cautious about sharing sensitive information, even in private groups.
- If something feels off, trust your instincts. Leaving a group is okay if it doesn't feel like a safe space.

## THE VALUE OF VIRTUAL FRIENDSHIPS

The friendships you cultivate online can be just as real and meaningful as those in person. These connections can offer support, laughter, and companionship, enriching your life in countless ways. They prove that we're never truly alone, no matter where we are. There's always someone just a message away who shares our passions, dreams, and challenges.

In this digital age, the world is our garden, ripe with opportunities for connection, growth, and discovery. So, go ahead, find your tribe online, and watch your garden of interests bloom into a vibrant community of friends and fellow enthusiasts.

## 8.2 BLOGGING: SHARING YOUR EXPERIENCES AND CONNECTING WITH READERS

Starting your blog is like opening a window into your world for others to peek through. It's a platform where your voice can soar, sharing stories, insights, and passions. Whether you're a gourmet in the kitchen, a wizard with knitting needles, or a wanderer on endless trails, a blog allows you to document your journey and connect with like-minded souls across the globe. Here's how to plant the seeds for a flourishing blog garden.

- **Choosing a Platform**: The first step is like picking the suitable soil for your garden; it must be nurturing and supportive. *WordPress*, *Blogger*, and *Squarespace* are popular choices, each with its tools and templates. Consider ease of use, customization options, and whether you can invest in a paid plan for additional features.
- **Crafting Your Space**: This is where you get to design your garden. Choose a blog design that reflects your personality and makes navigation easy for visitors. A clean, organized layout with easy-to-read fonts and a splash of color can make a difference.
- **Creating Content**: Now, what will you plant in your garden? Your posts are the blooms that will attract visitors. Write about what you love, what moves you, and what you've learned. Authenticity resonates, drawing readers who share your interests or appreciate your perspective.
- **Engaging Visuals**: Just as flowers add beauty to a garden, images and videos can enhance your blog posts. They break up text, illustrate points, and add a personal touch. You can use photos, create graphics, or source high-quality images from stock photo sites.

Next, let's talk about nurturing your garden so it grows and attracts visitors.

- **Building an Audience**: Like a garden that needs sunlight and water, your blog thrives on visibility and engagement. Share your posts on social media, join blogging networks, and engage with other bloggers by commenting on their posts. These actions help draw people to your blog and encourage them to stay and explore.

- **SEO Basics**: Understanding SEO (Search Engine Optimization) can ensure search engines easily find your blog. Use relevant keywords, create compelling post titles, and include links to other posts on your blog to improve your visibility.
- **Interacting with Readers**: When readers leave comments, consider them guests admiring your garden. Respond with gratitude and engage in conversation. This builds a community around your blog, encouraging readers to return and share your posts with others.

Now, let's touch on the more personal aspects of blogging.

- **The Therapeutic Aspects of Writing**: Blogging can be a form of therapy, offering a space to express thoughts, work through emotions, and reflect on experiences. Writing about challenges, triumphs, and the mundane moments of life can be incredibly healing. Sharing your journey can also provide comfort and connection to readers going through similar experiences.

Finally, for those looking to sprinkle a bit of fairy dust on their blogs.

- **Monetizing Your Blog**: If you're interested in turning your passion into profit, there are several paths you can explore. Popular methods include affiliate marketing, sponsored posts, and selling digital products or services related to your niche. Remember, authenticity is critical; endorse products and services that you genuinely believe in and are relevant to your audience.

## 8.3 ONLINE FORUMS, ENGAGING IN DISCUSSIONS ON SHARED INTERESTS

Blogging is more than just a hobby; it's a way to share your voice with the world, connect with a community, and even open doors to new opportunities. Like any garden, a blog requires care, patience, and love to grow. So, start planting your seeds today, and watch as your blog blossoms into a beautiful, thriving space that reflects your essence.

Exploring online forums is like entering a lively marketplace, filled with discussions on your favorite topics. Each forum, whether small and unique or large and diverse, provides a space for every enthusiast. Whether you're a seasoned gardener seeking the secret to perennial blooms or a tech enthusiast keen on the latest gadgets, there's a forum with your name on it. Let's explore the digital world together, finding places where your contributions add value and connect you with like-minded individuals.

### FINDING RELEVANT FORUMS

Discovering the right forum is like finding a book you can't put down. It's about matching your interests with a community that shares your enthusiasm. Here's how to begin this discovery:

- Start with a broad search using keywords related to your interests followed by the word "forum" or "discussion board." This simple method often leads to a variety of options.
- Consider forums hosted on platforms like Reddit, which houses thousands of subreddits on nearly every topic imaginable. Here, granularity is key; the more specific your interest, the more likely you are to find a dedicated community.
- Explore specialized directory websites that list forums by category. These can serve as curated gateways to forums that cater to niche interests.

Once you've landed on a few promising forums, take the time to lurk. Yes, lurk. It's about quietly observing the flow of conversation, the etiquette, and the community vibe. This step ensures you'll feel right at home when you join.

## PARTICIPATING IN DISCUSSIONS

Engaging in forum discussions is the heart of the experience, where you share, question, and debate. Here's how to do it gracefully:

- Prioritize quality over quantity. Thoughtful, well-articulated posts contribute more to the community than rapid-fire comments.
- Introduce yourself if the forum has a dedicated space for new members. A brief hello and a few words about your interests can go a long way in making connections.
- Always read the original post (OP) thoroughly before responding. This ensures your contribution is relevant and adds value to the discussion.
- Respect is paramount. Remember, behind every username is a person with feelings and opinions. Agree to disagree with dignity.

Remember, every post you make is a reflection of you. It's about building a reputation as a knowledgeable, respectful, and engaging community member.

## CREATING CONNECTIONS

Forums aren't just about exchanging information; they're fertile ground for friendships. These digital interactions often become real-world connections, enriching your life beyond the screen. Here's how to cultivate these connections:

- Look for members who consistently resonate with your thoughts and interests. Personal messages can be a great way to deepen conversations that started in public threads.
- Participate in or propose virtual meet-ups. Many forums organize online events, offering a live setting to interact with fellow members.
- If the forum organizes real-world meet-ups, consider joining. Meeting face-to-face can solidify friendships and add a new dimension to your forum experience.

Whether through shared laughter over a forum joke or a deep exchange on a topic close to your heart, these connections underscore the human aspect of online forums.

## LEARNING AND SHARING KNOWLEDGE

At its core, a forum is a living library, a collective repository of knowledge where every post has the potential to enlighten or inspire. Here's how to make the most of this educational aspect:

- Don't hesitate to ask questions, no matter how basic they might seem. Forums thrive on curiosity, and there's always someone willing to share insights.
- Offer your expertise generously. Whether it's solving a technical issue or recommending resources, your knowledge can be a lifeline for someone else.
- Stay updated on your interests by following threads and topics that matter to you. Many forums offer notification options to keep you in the loop.

In forums, each member is both teacher and student, engaged in a continuous cycle of learning and sharing. It's a dynamic that keeps the community vibrant, relevant, and invaluable.

As you navigate the colorful world of online forums, you'll discover more than just solutions to pressing questions or advice for your next project.

You'll discover a community that cheers on your successes, supports you through challenges, and, above all, shares your passions. This journey through the world of forums isn't just about what you take but also what you leave behind — the ideas you share, the connections you make, and the mark you imprint on the community. So jump in, contribute, and watch as these online interactions come together to create lasting bonds and shared memories.

## 8.4   VIDEO CONFERENCING: HOSTING VIRTUAL FAMILY REUNIONS

Gathering the entire family under one digital roof for a virtual reunion can turn an ordinary day into an extraordinary one. We live in a time where miles apart doesn't mean hearts apart, thanks to video conferencing. It's like opening your home's doors wide, inviting laughter, stories, and love without worrying about how everyone will fit. Here's a step-by-step guide to creating these memorable moments.

## ORGANIZING THE EVENT

First things first, getting everyone on the same page is crucial. This begins with picking a date and time that works for as many family members as possible. Consider different time zones and find a happy medium that allows everyone to join in comfortably:

- Use a poll or survey to decide the most convenient date and time.
- Choose a video conferencing platform familiar to most family

members. Platforms like ***Zoom***, ***Skype***, and ***Google Meet*** are user-friendly and allow significant group calls.

- Send out digital invitations with clear instructions on how to join the video call. Include a link to a quick tutorial for those who might need to become more familiar with the chosen platform.

## ACTIVITIES TO LIVEN UP THE REUNION

A well-planned virtual reunion can be as lively and engaging as an in-person gathering. The key is to have a mix of activities that cater to all ages and interests:

- **Walk Down Memory Lane**: Encourage family members to share old photos or home videos in advance. Create a slideshow to watch together during the reunion.
- **Online Games**: Opt for games that can be easily played over a video call, such as trivia, Pictionary, or family-friendly quiz games.
- **Talent Showcase**: Set up a virtual talent show where family members can sing, play an instrument, recite a poem, or show off a dance move.
- **Recipe Share**: Have each family branch share a favorite recipe. Pick one recipe and have each family prepare it in their kitchen during the reunion, turning it into a cook-along.

## ENSURING INCLUSIVITY

A successful family reunion is one where every member feels included and valued. This is especially important in a virtual setting where it's easy for quieter voices to get lost.

- Make sure everyone gets a chance to speak. Consider having a casual "master of ceremonies" who can gently guide the conversation and ensure everyone is included.

- Use the breakout room feature for larger families. This allows smaller groups to catch up in a more intimate setting before returning to the larger group.
- Provide instructions on muting and unmuting microphones to minimize background noise and make communication smoother.

## CAPTURING THE MOMENT

One of the advantages of a virtual reunion is the ease with which you can capture these moments for posterity.

- Take screenshots during the call. These digital snapshots can capture the laughter and smiles, serving as reminders of the day.
- If your platform allows, record the session (with everyone's consent). This is particularly special for moments like the talent showcase or the recipe share.
- After the event, compile these photos, videos, and shared recipes or stories into a digital family album. Online platforms allow you to create beautiful albums that can be shared with everyone and cherished for years.

In this age where technology brings us closer, a virtual family reunion is a beautiful way to strengthen bonds, share laughs, and create new memories. It's about turning pixels on a screen into a canvas that captures the heart and soul of your family, painting a picture of togetherness that transcends distance. With some planning, creativity, and love, these digital gatherings can become highlights of the year, eagerly anticipated by every family member.

## 8.5　ONLINE GAMING: CONNECTING THROUGH PLAY

In the vast expanse of the internet, gaming is a vibrant oasis where players from all walks of life converge, seeking adventure, camaraderie, and the thrill of victory. Picture it: a realm where age, location, and background fade into the background, replaced by shared objectives and the joy of play. Whether strategizing to conquer empires, solving puzzles to escape virtual rooms, or banding together to explore new worlds, online gaming offers a unique blend of entertainment and connection.

## CHOOSING GAMES TO PLAY TOGETHER

The first step in this digital adventure is selecting the correct game, which sets the stage for future experiences. The key here is variety — offering something for everyone, from fast-paced action games that get your heart racing to cerebral strategy games that challenge the mind. Consider games that support multiplayer modes, ensuring everyone can enjoy the fun. For families, co-op games where you can team up to achieve goals can be advantageous, fostering teamwork and cooperation.

- For strategy lovers, games like "*Civilization*" and "*Stardew Valley*" provide an immersive experience that demands planning and foresight.
- Puzzle games such as "*Portal 2*" and "*The Witness*" challenge players to think outside the box, perfect for those who enjoy solving complex problems.
- Action-adventure games like *"Fortnite"* and *"Minecraft"* cater to those seeking excitement and creativity, offering endless exploration and interaction.

## CREATING GAMING GROUPS

Once you've chosen your virtual battlefield, the next step is forming your gaming group, a digital squad united by common goals. This can be as simple as gathering friends and family or as expansive as joining online communities to meet new people. Many games offer built-in systems to create or join existing clans, making it easy to connect with fellow gamers. For a more organized approach, consider setting up regular gaming sessions, using tools like Discord or Slack to coordinate times and discuss strategies:

- Setting clear expectations regarding time commitment and participation can help ensure everyone is on the same page.
- Creating a dedicated group chat for your team can facilitate communication, allowing members to share tips, schedule gaming sessions, and bond over shared experiences.

## BENEFITS OF GAMING

The realm of online gaming is rich with benefits that extend far beyond mere entertainment. Engaging in these digital adventures can sharpen problem-solving skills and foster a spirit of teamwork as players work together to overcome challenges. Moreover, the social aspect of gaming cannot be understated; it's a powerful tool for building friendships and connecting with others who share your interests. For many, these virtual connections become a vital source of support and camaraderie.

- Cognitive benefits include enhanced multitasking abilities, improved memory, and quicker decision-making skills.
- Online gaming can serve as a stress reliever, offering an escape from the pressures of daily life and an outlet for relaxation and fun.

## STAYING SAFE IN ONLINE GAMING COMMUNITIES

While the digital gaming world offers countless opportunities for connection and growth, navigating it safely is paramount. Maintaining privacy and security in online gaming communities is crucial, as well as protecting personal information and ensuring a positive and respectful environment for all:

- Be cautious with personal information, sharing only what is necessary and using privacy settings to control who can see your profile and interact with you.
- Be mindful of online interactions, treat fellow gamers with respect, and avoid toxic behavior. Many games and platforms have reporting systems for inappropriate behavior; don't hesitate to use them.
- Educate yourself and others about online safety. Knowledge is power, and understanding the potential risks of online gaming can help you avoid them.

As we wrap up this exploration of online gaming, it's clear that these digital playgrounds offer much more than just a way to pass the time. They're gateways to new worlds, opportunities to learn and grow, and platforms for forging lasting connections. Whether strategizing over a game of chess, embarking on epic quests, or solving puzzles together, gaming brings us closer, bridging distances and breaking down barriers. So grab your controller, headset, or keyboard and dive into the adventure. The world of online gaming awaits, ready to connect us through the universal language of play.

**Here's a little fun:**

---

*Q: WHY DID THE COMPUTER GO TO THE DOCTOR?*

*A: BECAUSE IT HAD A VIRUS AND NEEDED "TECH SUPPORT"!*

# CHAPTER 9

# MAKING THE MOST OF YOUR COMMUNITY

*"Alone we can do so little; together we can do so much."*

### *HELEN KELLER*

Have you ever noticed how the best things in life, like a hearty laugh with an old friend, the serene beauty of a sunrise, or the crisp air on a fall morning, don't cost a dime? It's a gentle reminder that happiness doesn't always have a price tag. Let's focus on the treasures hidden within our communities in the spirit of  embracing life's simple joys. From laughter-filled evenings at local events to the enriching embrace of nature and the heartwarming connection of volunteering, this chapter is your guide to uncovering these gems, proving that the best experiences are often free.

## 9.1  DISCOVERING LOCAL EVENTS

Your neighborhood is a bustling hub of activity waiting to be explored. Here's how to stay in the loop:

- **Community Boards and Libraries**: These are goldmines for information on upcoming events. Next time you're returning a book or passing by a community bulletin board, take a moment to see what's posted.
- **Digital Platforms**: Websites and social media pages dedicated to your city or neighborhood often list local events. *Eventbrite* and *Facebook* Events are great places to start. Setting up alerts for your area can keep you informed without searching.
- **Local Newspapers**: They still exist and are packed with upcoming event listings. The weekend editions are vibrant with information.
- **Support your Candidate or Political Party:** If you are passionate about politics, why not volunteer to raise funds or set up a community event to support your candidate?

Attending these events, from art exhibits that spark your creativity to concerts that get your foot tapping, adds vibrancy to your life and supports local artists and performers.

## MAXIMIZING COMMUNITY RESOURCES

The local community center, library, or park is a treasure trove of free workshops, classes, and activities. Here's how to make the most of them:

- **Workshops and Classes**: Have you ever wanted to try your hand at pottery or learn a new dance style? Check out the offerings at your community center. You might be surprised at the variety of classes available at no cost.

- **Outdoor Activities**: Many parks organize free yoga sessions, nature walks, or bird-watching tours. It's a great way to stay active and connect with nature.
- **Public Libraries**: Beyond books, libraries often host author talks, book clubs, and educational seminars. These can be fantastic opportunities to learn something new and meet people with similar interests.

Participating in these activities enriches your life with new skills and experiences and strengthens your connection to the community.

## VOLUNTEERING FOR FREE ACCESS

Sometimes, the best way to enjoy an event is to be part of making it happen. Volunteering at local festivals, concerts, or art shows can offer you a behind-the-scenes look and free event access. Here's why it's worth considering:

- **Insider Experience**: As a volunteer, you see a different side of events, from the planning stages to the final applause. It's a unique learning experience with its own reward set.
- **Complimentary Access**: In exchange for your time and effort, you often get free admission to the event, not to mention any performances or exhibits it includes.
- **Community Impact**: Your contribution helps ensure the event's success, benefiting your local community and making these enriching experiences accessible to everyone. Plus you'll meet some new friends!

Whether guiding guests at an art exhibit or helping set up for a local concert, volunteering allows you to enjoy and contribute to your community's cultural landscape.

## BUILDING A SOCIAL CIRCLE

Attending free events and volunteering enriches your life with experiences and opens doors to new friendships. Here's how these activities can expand your social circle:

- **Shared Interests**: Events naturally attract people with common interests. Strike up a conversation about the art piece before you or the music genre being played. It's a natural icebreaker.
- **Volunteering Together**: Working alongside others towards a common goal fosters a sense of camaraderie and teamwork. Don't be surprised if you leave the event with a few new friends.
- **Regular Attendance**: Regularly attending events or volunteer activities increases your chances of running into familiar faces, gradually building a community of acquaintances and friends.

These community offerings are not just activities but doorways to new connections, shared experiences, and a more prosperous, vibrant life. They remind us that sometimes, the best things in life are free, waiting just around the corner for us to reach out and embrace them.

## 9.2  HOME ENTERTAINMENT: MOVIE NIGHTS AND GAME EVENINGS

In an era where the allure of digital screens is omnipresent, rediscovering the joy of home-based entertainment nurtures bonds with loved ones. It rekindles the simple pleasures that our bustling lives often sideline. Let's unwrap the delights of organizing movie nights, the resurgence of board games, the thrill of digital game nights, and the creativity involved in themed evenings, all of which promise memorable moments without straining your wallet.

## ORGANIZING MOVIE NIGHTS

Transforming your living space into a mini cinema is easier than you might think, and it's a fantastic way to bring everyone together. Start by selecting films that appeal to a broad audience, ensuring a mix caters to different tastes. Consider classics that never grow old, animated features that delight both the young and the young at heart, or documentaries that spark curiosity and conversation.

Setting the scene is pivotal:

- Arrange comfortable seating that mimics the cozy corners of a theater. Think pillows on the floor, bean bags, or rearranging furniture to create an inviting layout.
- Dim the lights or drape soft fairy lights for that cinematic ambiance.
- Remember the snacks! Popcorn is a given, but why not add a twist with homemade seasonings or an array of finger foods that keep the palette as engaged as the storyline?

## FUN WITH BOARD GAMES AND PUZZLES

Board games and puzzles have made a roaring comeback, becoming staples for engaging and cost-effective evenings. They're entertainment and brain teasers that enhance problem-solving skills and foster teamwork. From strategy-heavy games that demand critical thinking to lighthearted options that have everyone in stitches, the key is variety.

Here's how to make board game and puzzle nights a hit:

- Keep a selection that caters to different group sizes and attention spans. Quick card games are great for short bursts of fun, while longer board games can make an evening fly by.
- Encourage everyone to take turns picking the game. It ensures variety and keeps everyone invested.
- For puzzles, consider a communal approach where a puzzle is left on a table, allowing family members to add pieces over time. It's a shared project that everyone contributes to, piece by piece.

## DIGITAL GAME NIGHTS

The digital realm offers a multiplayer game playground that connects friends and family, whether in the same room or miles apart. Platforms like *Steam, PlayStation Network*, and *Xbox Live* provide access to many games that support multiplayer modes, many of which are free or reasonably priced.

To ensure these digital game nights are a blast, consider the following:

- Opt for games that match the group's interest. Whether adventure quests, sports simulations, or classic board games in digital format, the suitable game can keep everyone engaged for hours.
- Use voice chat features to keep the banter going. It adds a personal touch, making the virtual experience feel more connected.
- Rotate the choice of games. Allowing different participants to pick the game each time keeps the lineup fresh and inclusive.

## CREATIVE THEMED EVENINGS

Themed evenings add extra excitement to home entertainment, turning a regular night into an event. The theme could be as simple as a color, a specific decade, or inspired by the cuisine of a particular country. The idea is to weave this theme through every evening aspect, from the dress code and decorations to the activities and food.

Here's a blueprint for success:

- Choose a theme that sparks excitement. A '70s disco night, a pirate-themed adventure, or a 'Around the World' tasting evening can set the stage for an unforgettable experience.
- Get everyone involved in the preparations. Assign tasks based on interests — someone could create a themed playlist, another could handle decorations, and so forth.
- Plan activities that align with the theme. For a detective-themed evening, a murder mystery game could be the highlight. Trivia or video games centered around sports could keep the competitive spirit alive for a sports-themed night.
- Encourage themed snacks and drinks. For a Mexican fiesta, think tacos, guacamole, and margaritas. A '60s evening could be complemented with fondue and classic cocktails.

Each of these elements, from movie nights that bring the magic of cinema home, board games that challenge and amuse, digital game nights that bridge distances with laughter, to themed evenings that transport you to another world, serve as reminders that joy doesn't have to come with a hefty price tag. It's about creativity, shared experiences, and the warmth of spending time with those who matter most.

## 9.3  NATURE'S BOUNTY: HIKING AND PICNICKING IN NATURE RESERVES

Strolling through the lush greenery of your local nature reserve, you can't help but feel a sense of peace over you. Every step on the trail is a gentle reminder of the world's natural beauty, a canvas of vibrant colors and textures that change with the seasons. In these moments, surrounded by the symphony of rustling leaves and chirping birds, we find a profound connection to the earth beneath our feet. Hiking and picnicking in these natural sanctuaries offer not just an escape from the daily grind but a way to engage with the environment in a meaningful, enjoyable manner.

## EXPLORING THE GREAT OUTDOORS

The call of the wild is not just an echo from distant, untamed lands; it resonates through the heart of our local parks and nature reserves. These spaces are open invitations to lace up your hiking boots and set out on an adventure that rejuvenates both body and soul. The trails offer varying difficulty levels, catering to seasoned and casual walkers alike. Here's how to make the most of these natural pathways:

- Start small. If you're new to hiking, select shorter trails that will be manageable. This builds confidence and stamina for longer treks.
- Stay hydrated and pack light. A reusable water bottle and a small backpack with essentials keep you comfortable without weighing you down.
- Use trail maps and signage to navigate. Many parks offer downloadable maps or interactive apps to help you find your way.

The health benefits of regular outdoor activity are vast, from improved cardiovascular health to reduced stress levels. Moreover, the sheer joy of discovering a panoramic view after a challenging climb is a reward.

## PICNICKING ON A BUDGET

Pairing a hike with a picnic transforms a simple outing into a memorable experience. The art of picnicking, however, lies not in extravagance but in preparation and simplicity. With creativity, you can create a spread that delights the taste buds without emptying your wallet. Here are some tips for a budget-friendly feast:

- Plan your menu around seasonal produce. Fruits and vegetables in season are cheaper and at their peak flavor.
- Homemade treats like sandwiches, wraps, or salads are cost-effective and can be tailored to your dietary preferences.
- Freeze bottles of water or juice overnight. They'll keep your food chilled and provide a refreshing drink once thawed.

A picnic, after all, is less about the food and more about enjoying a meal in the embrace of nature, surrounded by the beauty and tranquility of the outdoors.

## FORAGING AND NATURE WALKS

Imagine walking through the woods, basket in hand, foraging for wild edibles. It's an activity that ties us back to our ancestral roots, offering a unique way to engage with the natural world. Foraging for wild foods like berries, nuts, and mushrooms adds an element of exploration and learning to your nature walks, but it requires knowledge and respect for the environment. Here's how to get started:

- Educate yourself. Join guided foraging walks or workshops led by experts. Books and apps on local flora can also be valuable resources.
- Always forage responsibly. Harvest in a way that ensures plants can regenerate and never take more than you need.
- Be sure to identify wild food before consuming it to avoid poisonous species.

Foraging enriches your diet with natural, healthy foods and fosters a deeper appreciation for the biodiversity of your local ecosystem.

## RESPONSIBLE ENJOYMENT OF NATURE

As we immerse ourselves in the beauty of nature reserves, it's crucial to tread lightly, ensuring our actions don't disrupt these delicate ecosystems. The principles of "Leave No Trace" are guidelines that help preserve the natural integrity of outdoor spaces for future generations. Here's how to practice responsible enjoyment of nature:

- Stick to marked trails to avoid harming native plants and wildlife habitats.
- Pack out what you pack in. Leave the area as you found it, or even cleaner if you come across litter left by others.
- Respect wildlife. Observe from a distance; never feed animals as it disrupts their natural foraging habits.

By adhering to these practices, we contribute to conserving these precious natural resources, ensuring they remain vibrant and accessible for all who seek solace and adventure in the great outdoors.

In essence, the allure of nature reserves lies not just in their scenic beauty but in the myriad ways they allow us to connect with the environment and each other. Whether it's the solitary piece of a solo hike, the shared joy of a family picnic, the thrill of discovering edible treasures along the trail, or the satisfaction of leaving no trace behind, these experiences enrich our lives profoundly.

## 9.4   SKILL SWAPPING: TEACHING AND LEARNING NEW SKILLS FOR FREE

In a world of hidden talents and untapped knowledge, skill swapping is a beacon of communal learning and sharing. Picture a group of neighbors, each bringing a unique set of skills to the table, ready to exchange wisdom without the exchange of money. From the culinary arts to the intricacies of home repair, these sessions become a vibrant marketplace of knowledge, fostering a sense of community and mutual growth.

## SETTING UP SKILL SWAP SESSIONS

Organizing a skill swap event in your community can transform neighbors' interactions, turning acquaintances into lifelong learners and teachers. The initial step involves gauging interest and identifying the skills available within the community. A simple flyer at the local café or a post on a neighborhood social media page can kickstart this discovery process.

Once you've gathered a group eager to share their knowledge, consider the logistics:

- Find a venue to accommodate your group. Community centers, public parks, or spacious backyards can be ideal spots.
- Schedule sessions at times that work for most people, perhaps weekends or evenings, ensuring maximum participation.
- Create a sign-up system where participants can list the skills they're willing to teach and those they want to learn. This helps in planning and matching skill sets effectively.

The beauty of these sessions lies in their flexibility and the organic exchange of knowledge that unfolds. Each meeting can be a deep dive into a specific skill, with hands-on demonstrations and Q&A sessions that enrich the learning experience for everyone involved.

## LEVERAGING ONLINE PLATFORMS

In today's digital age, the potential for skill swapping extends far beyond the confines of local communities. Online platforms and social media groups offer a vast, untapped reservoir of knowledge, connecting individuals from diverse backgrounds and geographies.

Platforms like *Nextdoor* or *Meetup* allow you to create or join groups focused on skill swapping. Here, you can organize virtual learning sessions, leveraging video conferencing tools to conduct workshops or demonstrations. These online gatherings not only break down geographical barriers but also enable the sharing highly specialized skills that might be rare in your immediate vicinity.

Tips for successful online skill swap sessions include:

- Ensure clear communication about the time and platform for the virtual meet-up.
- Prepare materials or resources that participants can refer to during and after the session.
- Encourage interaction and questions, making the online experience as engaging and collaborative as possible.

This digital approach to skill swapping opens up a world of possibilities where learning and teaching can happen across time zones, bringing together a global community of curious minds and eager teachers.

## BARTERING SKILLS FOR SERVICES

Taking the concept of skill swapping a step further, bartering emerges as a powerful way to exchange services, fostering an environment of support and reciprocity. Imagine trading a photography session for a series of personal training sessions or offering gardening help in exchange for home-cooked meals. This trade system strengthens community bonds and underscores the value of skills over monetary transactions.

To facilitate a successful swap, consider the following:

- Clearly define the scope and expectations of the exchange to ensure both parties agree.
- Keep track of commitments and schedules, treating the swap professionally as a paid service.
- View each exchange as an opportunity to build trust and

rapport within your community, laying the groundwork for future collaborations.

Bartering revives an age-old practice of trade that relies on trust, respect, and the intrinsic value of skills, enriching the community fabric with every exchange.

## DOCUMENTING AND SHARING KNOWLEDGE

The ripple effect of skill swapping is magnified when the knowledge exchanged is documented and shared with a broader audience. Creating a blog, a YouTube channel, or a community newsletter dedicated to showcasing the skills and lessons from each session preserves the knowledge and inspires others to join the movement.

Here are ways to effectively document and share the wealth of information:

- Take photos or videos during live sessions, capturing the essence of the learning experience.
- Encourage participants to contribute to the content creation, sharing their insights, tips, and reflections on the skills they've learned or taught.
- Distribute the content through accessible channels, ensuring it reaches community members and a wider audience interested in skill swapping.

**Just for Kicks and Giggles:**

---

Q: WHY DID THE COMMUNITY CENTER GET A TROPHY?

A: BECAUSE IT WAS THE "SOCIAL NETWORK" CHAMPION!

---

# CHAPTER 10

# BUDGET TRAVEL HACKS FOR THE SAVVY TRAVELER

---

*"Not all those who wander are lost."*

**J.R.R TOLKIEN**

---

Many people plan to travel during retirement. Whether you're a novice or an experienced globe-trotter, the world has many unique destinations, and there's no way you could visit them all. Traveling alone or with a packaged tour is a great option. Or, if you have a travel buddy, it's fun to plan your trips together and create a shared photo album with friends and family afterward.

My husband and I are great travel buddies, but there are still so many places that we want to see! To narrow down and prioritize, we each wrote our separate "bucket list destinations" and shared our lists. The destinations that made both of our lists stayed on our "Couples Travel Bucket List." It's surprising and fun!

For more budget-friendly hacks and travel destinations in North America, South America, Asia, the Middle East, and Europe, you can check out our free ebook using this QR Code (ADD QR CODE which links to the Landing Page; also add Landing Page URL)

## EXPLORING THE WORLD WITHOUT BREAKING THE BANK

Budget travel is not just for college students: It's a smart way to travel, if you do your research and have the right attitude. Travel doesn't have to drain your savings account. With savvy planning and a willingness to go against the grain, you can explore the world's wonders without breaking the bank. Here's how to stretch those travel dollars further, ensuring your retirement adventures are rich in experiences, not expenses.

If you use a travel agent to plan your trips, mention that you must stay within a specific budget and use all senior discounts. There are several great packaged tour operators specifically for people 55 and over. Try Road Scholars for imaginative itineraries with fellow retirees!

## TRAVELING OFF-PEAK

Choosing when to travel can significantly impact your budget. Off-peak seasons offer a twofold benefit: not only are flights and accommodations often cheaper, but destinations are less crowded, allowing for a more relaxed exploration. For instance, visiting Europe in the fall or late winter can lead to significant savings compared to summer. Plus, the milder weather can make sightseeing more enjoyable.

- Research your desired destination to determine its off-peak periods.
- Be flexible with your travel dates. Sometimes, flying mid-week can offer additional savings.

- Keep an eye on travel alerts or deals. Many travel websites offer notifications for discounted rates during off-peak times.

Off-peak and shoulder seasons offer a twofold benefit: not only are flights and accommodations often cheaper, but destinations during off-peak seasons vary by destination but generally fall outside significant holidays and school vacations. During these times, you can enjoy several benefits:

- **Lower Costs**: Airlines and hotels often reduce prices to attract travelers during slower periods.
- **Fewer Crowds**: With fewer tourists, you can explore attractions more comfortably and often get a more authentic feel for your destination.
- **Pleasant Weather**: In many places, the shoulder seasons (spring and fall) offer mild weather, perfect for sightseeing.

For example, visiting Europe in the fall can mean lower airfares, cheaper accommodations, and shorter lines at popular attractions like the Eiffel Tower or the Colosseum. Similarly, Caribbean islands are often less expensive and less crowded during the late spring and early summer.

**Utilizing Budget Travel Resources**

In today's digital age, many resources are available to help travelers find the best deals. An app or website is designed to save you money on everything from accommodation to flights and activities:

- **Accommodations**: Platforms like *Airbnb*, *Hostelworld*, and *Booking.com* offer a range of lodging options for every budget. Consider staying in hostels, guesthouses, or budget hotels to cut down on costs.
- **Flights**: Find the cheapest flights using flight comparison tools like *Skyscanner* or *Google Flights*. Setting up alerts for specific routes can help you snag a deal when prices drop.

- **Activities**: Websites like *Groupon* or local tourism boards often have discounts or packages for attractions and tours.

Remember, the key is comparing prices across different platforms before booking. Direct bookings with hotels or airlines can be cheaper.

## EMBRACING SLOW TRAVEL

Slow travel is about immersing yourself in the local culture, cuisine, and community rather than rushing from one tourist spot to another. Staying in one place for extended periods allows you to:

- Negotiate better rates for longer-term accommodations.
- Discover hidden gems that aren't in the guidebooks, often at a lower cost.
- Save on transportation by walking or using local transit instead of hopping on flights or long-distance trains.

This approach saves money and enriches your travel experience, allowing you to form deeper connections with the places you visit.

## LEVERAGING SENIOR DISCOUNTS

Remember to underestimate the power of a senior discount. Many travel-related companies offer reduced rates for seniors, from flights and trains to museum entry fees and national park passes. Here's how to ensure you don't miss out:

- Always ask about AARP and senior discounts when booking flights, accommodations, or activities. Even if it's not advertised, many places offer them upon request.
- Look into senior discount cards or programs specific to the country you're visiting. For example, the U.S. National Parks Service offers a lifetime pass for seniors at a nominal fee, providing access to over 2,000 federal recreation sites.

- Public transportation in many cities also reduces seniors' fares, making city exploration more affordable.

## OTHER TIPS FOR STAYING ON A BUDGET

Here's a cheat sheet for traveling without breaking the bank:

- **Plan Your Travel Dates:** Traveling off-peak, aka during the shoulder seasons, can help you avoid crowds and find lower prices on accommodations and flights.
- **Choose Your Destinations Wisely**: Focus on a specific region or city to explore in-depth rather than trying to cover too much ground, which can be costly and time-consuming.
- **Look for Budget Accommodations:** Consider staying in hostels, budget hotels, or vacation rentals like Airbnb. Camping is also popular and affordable in national parks and wilderness areas. You'll meet many younger people and learn about the local attractions!
- **Take Advantage of Public Transportation**: Many cities have efficient public transit systems, which can be a cost-effective way to get around. For longer distances, consider taking buses or trains, like those operated by VIA Rail, which offers scenic routes across the country.
- **Eat Like a Local:** Save money by shopping at local markets and cooking your meals, or look for affordable dining options like food trucks, diners, and small local restaurants. You'll want to explore the diverse culinary scene, so there's plenty to explore without breaking the bank.
- **Enjoy Free and Low-Cost Attractions**: Many cities and towns offer free or low-cost attractions, such as public parks, museums with free admission days, and cultural festivals. Nature is one of life's biggest draws, so take advantage of the many hiking trails, lakes, and scenic drives that are accessible for free.

- **Travel Insurance**: Don't forget to purchase travel insurance, as it can save you from unexpected expenses due to medical emergencies or other unforeseen events.
- **Stay Informed and Safe:** Keep an eye on travel advisories and weather conditions, especially if planning outdoor activities or traveling to wintery destinations.
- **Bargain Wisely**: In markets and with street vendors, it's common to haggle over prices. However, do so respectfully and remember that a small amount might mean more to the seller than to you.
- **Use a Refillable Water Bottle**: Tap water in many countries is not always safe to drink, so bring a refillable water bottle with a filter to save money on bottled water and reduce plastic waste.
- **Look for Discount Cards:** Many cities offer tourist cards that provide free or discounted access to public transport, museums, and attractions, which can be a great way to save money if you visit many sites.
- **Shop at Local Markets**: Local markets often offer better prices for groceries and souvenirs than tourist-oriented shops. You can find fresh produce, cheese, and other local products at a fraction of the cost.

Traveling on a budget means more than just saving a few dollars; it's about making the most of every moment, finding joy in the simple pleasures, and discovering that the actual value of travel lies in the experiences, not the expenditures. It's a reminder that adventures are waiting around every corner, ready to unfold for those who seek them with an open heart and a keen eye for the road less traveled.

**Heres a joke to brighten your day:**

---

Q: WHY DID THE BUDGET TRAVELER BREAK UP WITH THEIR SUITCASE?

A: IT HAD TOO MUCH EMOTIONAL BAGGAGE AND LITTLE ROOM FOR SOUVENIRS!

# WHAT'S NEXT?

---

*"Life begins at the end of your comfort zone."*

**NEALE DONALD WALSCH**

---

Well, my fabulous soon-to-be retirees and vibrant golden-agers, we are at the end of our expedition into reimagining what retirement could look like. It's like finding the last jigsaw puzzle piece under the couch, right? We've traveled together through the world of apps and tablets, dipped our toes into water aerobics, and even had a whirl at organizing movie nights that could rival any cinema experience.

Let's take a moment to celebrate this journey. We've discovered that retirement is not the final curtain call but rather the grand opening of an opera where you're both the star and the director. We've explored everything from snapping the perfect photo with your smartphone to sinking your hands into garden soil and the thrill of penning your life stories or fictional tales that could give J.K. Rowling a run for her money.

The key takeaway? Retirement is your canvas, and you've got an entire palette of colors to play with. Whether learning a new language, mastering the art of sourdough bread, or finally figuring out how to play 'Stairway to Heaven' on the guitar, the possibilities are as limitless as episodes in a Netflix series you can't stop binge-watching.

I'm here to nudge you (gently, of course) to take that first step. Pick just one activity or idea from our treasure chest that sparked a little fire in your belly and give it a go. Remember, Rome wasn't built in a day, nor is the dream retirement lifestyle: small steps, my friends, small steps.

Embrace change and growth like you would an old friend popping by unannounced. Retirement is your time to shine, explore uncharted territories, get lost, and find new paths occasionally. It's a dynamic, ever-evolving chapter of your life ripe with opportunities for personal growth and exploration.

So, what's next? I invite you (yes, you with the adventurous spirit and the youthful heart) to grab a pen and paper (or your tablet; we're tech-savvy here) and start sketching out your personalized retirement plan. It might be a good time to write down some "bucket list items" of things you want to try! Use our journey through this book as your springboard and fill your plan with activities, goals, and dreams that resonate with you. Whether it's conquering the highest peaks or the art of doing absolutely nothing in style, make it uniquely yours.

As we part ways, remember this: your retirement is a blank book, and you're the author holding the pen. You can fill it with stories of adventure, learning, love, and laughter. So, here's to your vibrant, purpose-filled, and utterly fantastic retirement ahead. Cheers to you and your next great adventure!

# KEEPING THE GAME ALIVE!

Now that you have all the tools to make the most of your retirement, it's time to share your newfound wisdom and guide other readers to the same resources.

By sharing your review about "Fun Things to Do in Retirement" on Amazon, you'll help fellow readers discover how they can add excitement and joy to their golden years and keep the spirit of adventure alive.

Click Here to Leave a Review

Your feedback makes a difference, and we're grateful for your contribution to keeping the retirement game alive and thriving!

Thank you for reading and reviewing my book! If you would like a signed copy please email me at Rhondahill00@yahoo.com

Here's to your exciting retirement!

*Rhonda*

# REFERENCES

- Smartphone Photography: The Essential Guide (+ 15 Tips). (n.d.). Digital Photography School. https://digital-photography-school.com/mobile-phone-photography-beginner-tips/
- 8 Great Travel Apps for Seniors. (n.d.). Torrance Memorial. https://www.torrancememorial.org/healthy-living/blog/8-great-travel-apps-for-seniors/
- How To Keep Seniors Safe in the Digital Age: A Social Media Safety Guide for Seniors. (n.d.). All About Cookies. https://allaboutcookies.org/social-media-safety-for-seniors
- The 8 Best Learning Apps of 2024. Lifewire. https://www.lifewire.com/best-learning-apps-417635717 *Places to Get Audiobooks for Free Online:* https://www.rd.com/list/download-and-listen-to-free-audiobooks/
- Best Brain Games and Apps to Keep Seniors' Minds Sharp. (n.d.). A Place for Mom. https://www.aplaceformom.com/caregiver-resources/articles/products-to-keep-the-mind-sharp
- *10 Best Free Music-Making Software for Beginners [2024]* https://www.movavi.com/learning-portal/free-music-making-software.html
- 11 Troubleshooting Tips for Better Video Calls. (n.d.). WeBoost. https://www.weboost.com/blog/how-does-video-conferencing-work-troubleshooting-tips-to-consider
- *Health Benefits of Water Aerobics for Seniors* https://bethesda-health.org/blog/2017/07/28/health-benefits-water-aerobics-seniors/
- OpenAI. *(2024). ChatGPT (4) [Large language model]. https://chat.openai.com - Illustrations*
- Author(s). (n.d.). Health benefits of tai chi. *PMC - NCBI.* https://www.ncbi.nlm.nih.gov/pmc/articles/PMC9844554/
- National Institute on Aging. (n.d.). Safety tips for exercising outdoors for older adults. *National Institute on Aging.* https://www.nia.nih.gov/health/exercise-and-physical-activity/safety-tips-exercising-outdoors-older-adults
- Author(s). (n.d.). Effects of dance therapy on cognitive and mental health in older adults. *BMC Geriatrics.* https://bmcgeriatr.biomedcentral.com/articles/10.1186/s12877-023-04406-y
- 12Oaks Senior Living. (n.d.). The benefits of bird watching for seniors. *12Oaks Senior Living.* https://12oaks.net/bird-watching-for-seniors/
- Take Me Fishing. (n.d.). Everything you need to start fishing. *Take Me Fishing.* https://www.takemefishing.org/how-to-fish/fishing-resources-events/everything-you-need-to-start-fishing/

- AARP. (n.d.). 7 gardening tools that reduce joint and wrist pain. *AARP*. https://www.aarp.org/home-family/your-home/info-2020/gardening-tools-comfort.html
- The Pioneer Woman. (n.d.). 20 best scenic drives in the US for an epic road trip. *The Pioneer Woman*. https://www.thepioneerwoman.com/home-lifestyle/g44795410/best-scenic-drives/
- Seabury Life. (n.d.). Why creative activities matter for seniors. *Seabury Life*. https://seaburylife.org/why-creative-activities-matter-for-seniors/
- Draw Paint Academy. (n.d.). Painting for beginners - A 7-step guide to get you started. *Draw Paint Academy*. https://drawpaintacademy.com/painting-for-beginners/
- Manzanita Press. (n.d.). Voices of wisdom - 50+ writing classes for seniors. *Manzanita Press*. https://manzapress.com/events-2023/voices-of-wisdom-55writing-classes-for-seniors/
- HGTV. (n.d.). 70 DIY decor projects to craft this weekend. *HGTV*. https://www.hgtv.com/design/make-and-celebrate/handmade/diy-decor-projects-to-craft-this-weekend-pictures
- Seasons Retirement. (n.d.). 10 amazing benefits of lifelong learning for older adults. *Seasons Retirement*. https://seasonsretirement.com/benefits-of-lifelong-learning/
- StoryPoint. (n.d.). Online learning for seniors: 6 of the best free resources. *StoryPoint*. https://www.storypoint.com/resources/health-wellness/online-learning-for-seniors/
- Book Riot. (n.d.). How to start book clubs for seniors: Your guide. *Book Riot*. https://bookriot.com/book-clubs-for-seniors/
- Seniority. (n.d.). 9 musical instruments that seniors can easily learn. *Seniority*. https://seniority.in/blog/9-musical-instruments-that-seniors-can-easily-learn
- Mayo Clinic Health System. (n.d.). 3 health benefits of volunteering. *Mayo Clinic Health System*. https://www.mayoclinichealthsystem.org/hometown-health/speaking-of-health/3-health-benefits-of-volunteering
- Golden Carers. (n.d.). Hobby clubs activity ideas for seniors & the elderly. *Golden Carers*. https://www.goldencarers.com/hobby-clubs/
- 14 Best Senior-friendly Travel Groups. (n.d.). Travel + Leisure. Retrieved from https://www.travelandleisure.com/trip-ideas/senior-travel/best-travel-groups-for-seniors
- Senior Fitness - West Side Programs and Classes. (n.d.). Retrieved from https://ymcanyc.org/locations/west-side-ymca/programs-and-classes/health-fitness/senior-fitness
- Blogging for Seniors: How to Start a Blog in Retirement. (2021, October 26). Feisty Side of Fifty. Retrieved from https://feistysideoffifty.com/2021/10/26/blogging-for-seniors-how-to-start-a-blog-in-retirement/
- Technology for Seniors: The Benefits of Video Games and ... (n.d.). The

Goodman Group Blog. Retrieved from https://blog.thegoodmangroup.com/
best-video-games-for-seniors

- The Senior's Guide to Online Safety. (n.d.). ConnectSafely. Retrieved from
  https://connectsafely.org/seniors-guide-to-online-safety/
- 14 Fun Virtual Family Reunion Ideas, Games & Activities. (n.d.).
  TeamBuilding. Retrieved from https://teambuilding.com/blog/virtual-
  family-reunion
- 8 Resources for Finding Free Things to Do in Your Area. (2014, July 22).
  Money. Retrieved from https://money.usnews.com/money/blogs/my-money/
  2014/07/22/8-resources-for-finding-free-things-to-do-in-your-area
- 10 Board Games to Help Seniors Battle Boredom and Reap.....(n.d.).
  [Publisher]. Retrieved from [URL]
- U.S. News & World Report. (n.d.). The cheapest places to retire abroad on
  $1K per month. Retrieved from https://money.usnews.com/money/
  retirement/baby-boomers/articles/the-cheapest-places-to-retire-abroad-on-1-
  000-per-month
- The Beginner's Guide to Foraging. (n.d.). Backpacker. Retrieved from
  https://www.backpacker.com/skills/foraging/

Printed in Great Britain
by Amazon

43065207R00086